2/8/84

THE TIMEX SINCLAIR 2068

What Can You Do With It?

Roger Valentine

Recreational Computing Series

A Wiley Press Book

John Wiley & Sons, Inc.

New York • Chichester • Brisbane • Toronto • Singapore

Library of Congress Cataloging in Publication Data

Valentine, Roger, 1949-
The Timex Sinclair 2068.

1. Timex Sinclair 2068 (Computer)—Programming.
I. Title.
QA76.8.T49V34 1983 001.64 83-5086
ISBN 0-471-88300-X (pbk.)

Printed in the United States of America

83 84 85 10 9 8 7 6 5 4 3 2 1

Contents

Preface *vii*

1 Five Easy Pieces *1*
Simple starters

2 Play It, Sam *11*
Computer games

3 Not Just Your Plaything *25*
Serious applications

4 Down Memory Lane *43*
Investigating the Timex Sinclair memory map

5 The Very Pulse of the Machine *59*
Machine Code routines

6 Interlude *69*
Totally silly programs

7 A Matter of Routine *77*
Useful subroutines

8 Art for Art's Sake *87*
Music and graphics

9 Under the Spreading Chestnut Tree *97*
Old favorites

10 Play It Again Sam *107*
More games

Preface

Who can use this book?

- A first-time computer buyer eager to learn the fundamentals of computer usage and programming.
- A games and graphics enthusiast who wants to use the high resolution color graphics.
- A person who's buying up to the Timex Sinclair 2068 because of the advanced range of features and the competitive prices.
- A business user attracted by the portability and 48K memory available.

You may be one of these people described above or have a Timex Sinclair 2068 Computer for reasons of your own. No matter what the reason, there are both useful and exciting programs in this book for you to use.

The programs are grouped into ten sections:

1. "Five Easy Pieces" are short, easy to enter programs designed to acquaint you with the Timex Sinclair, and introduce you to its character set, color, sound, and timing functions.

2. "Play It Sam" takes you into the world of computer games—moving graphics, arcade games as well as more sedate intellectual exercises.

3. "Not Just Your Plaything" is the other side of the coin. Serious applications including, of course, business programs.

4. "Down Memory Lane" is for the computer enthusiast, and is a collection of programs investigating the contents of the Timex Sinclair's memory.

5. "The Very Pulse of the Machine" is a selection of machine code routines. As well as mnemonic and decimal listings, each

routine is accompanied by a Basic program enabling the code to be loaded very simply.

6. From the sublime to the ridiculous, "Interlude" is a collection of utterly trivial programs to keep you entertained for minutes on end.

7. "A Matter of Routine" does not consist of programs at all, but of subroutines which you can adapt for use in programs of your own.

8. "Art for Art's Sake" is just that. Pictures and sound for your enjoyment.

9. "Under the Spreading Chestnut Tree" is a rather derogatory title for a collection of computer classics (well all right then, "chestnuts"), without which no program library would be complete.

10. Finally, you didn't think I would leave out the "Space" games, did you? These are in the last section "Play It Again Sam."

N.B. All of the programs will run in 16K, except "Invoicing," "Sales Ledger", and machine code "Pages" which require 48K.

LISTING CONVENTIONS

The following table has been printed using a PET dot matrix printer, the same as the one which was used for the program listings.

To avoid errors when keying in the programs, please ensure that you can distinguish between these characters:

```
1  = Number one
I  = Upper case letter I
l  = Lower case letter L
0  = Number zero
O  = Upper case letter O
o  = Lower case letter O
q  = Lower case letter Q
a  = Lower case letter A
() = Brackets
<> = Less than; greater than
"" = The 'null string' (Two consecutive quotation marks)
" "= Quote; space; quote
```

On the rare occasions where a string of two or more spaces is required, a REM statement has been included to indicate the number of spaces (if this is critical). All graphics characters (including User Defined Graphics) have been obtained by using the appropriate CHR$ command, so there are no strange graphics to decipher in the listings.

All variable names have been listed in lower case. All keywords are in upper case.

All programs contain a line number 9000, which is usually in the form:

```
9000 SAVE "TITLE" LINE 0
```

When you have keyed in a program, enter GO TO 9000 and it will be SAVEd in such a way that it will "auto run" when LOADed.

1

Five Easy Pieces

- LARGE CHARACTERS
- CHR TEST
- ATTR TABLE
- PIANO
- CLOCK

LARGE CHARACTERS

The first two programs are both concerned with investigating the Timex Sinclair Character Set.

The entire Character Set, which is listed in the Timex Sinclair manual, can be divided into five sections:

> **CHR$ 0 to CHR$ 31: Control Characters.** These are not characters in the everyday sense of the word, as they are not themselves printed on the screen. They affect such things as the color and TAB position of the next character which is to be printed.
>
> **CHR$ 32 to CHR$ 127: "Normal" Characters.** With the exception of the English pound symbol, this is the famous ASCII character set which is used by most personal computers.
>
> **CHR$ 128 to CHR$ 143: Sinclair Graphics.**
>
> **CHR$ 144 to CHR$ 164: User Defined Graphics.**
>
> **CHR$ 165 to CHR$ 255: "Composite" Characters.** Keywords, etc., which all have a specific function, but which are represented on screen by a combination of two or more "normal" characters.

The first program considers just the "normal" part of the character set, and examines how the characters are stored in ROM by printing each character 64 times its usual size.

The characters are stored in ROM at an address pointed to by the System Variable CHARS (see line 10), and are stored in exactly the same way as User Defined Graphics, i.e., eight bytes defining the pixel-pattern of each character.

These eight bytes are identified in line 25, and converted to binary form (BITs) in line 40. Each BIT, which would normally be used to signify that a single pixel is to be plotted or *not-plotted,* is then used to print an ENTIRE CHARACTER; either a black square (CHR$ 143) if the bit=1 or a white square (CHR$ 144) if the bit=0.

The purpose of the User Defined Graphic character in this program is to create a *grid* so that you can see exactly how each character is formed. You might find it useful when designing your own characters to study exactly how Timex Sinclair designed theirs.

LARGE CHARACTERS

```
5 RESTORE : FOR j=0 TO 7:  READ a: POKE USR
       CHR$ 144+j,a: NEXT j
10 LET c=PEEK 23606+256*PEEK 23607+256
15 FOR j=0 TO 95: CLS : PRINT AT 4,20;"CHR$ ";j+32;" ";
       CHR$ (j+32)
20 FOR p=0 TO 7
25 LET byte=PEEK (c+p+j*8)
30 PRINT AT p,15;byte
35 FOR l=1 TO 8
40 LET x=INT (byte/2): LET bit=byte-2*x: LET byte=x
45 PRINT AT p,9-l;CHR$ (144-bit)
50 NEXT l
55 NEXT p
60 IF j<>95 THEN PRINT AT 15,0;"Press any key for next
       character": PAUSE 0
65 NEXT j: STOP
100 DATA 255,129,129,129,129,129,129,255
9000 SAVE "CHR" LINE 0
```

CHR TEST

What better way to familiarize yourself with the Timex Sinclair character set than with a simple game which tests your knowledge of the CODE for each character.

The program draws a highly stylized Guy Fawkes-type bomb, with the fuse rapidly burning away. It also prints a random character, and you have a few seconds to enter the correct CODE number to defuse the bomb.

At first you will probably fail miserably, even with the help of the Timex Sinclair manual, but after a while you should find the game becoming easier as you gradually learn the ASCII part of the character set, and eventually the graphics and "composite" parts as well.

(For obvious reasons, the program does *not* select from either the Control Characters or the User Defined Graphics.)

The most interesting feature of the program is the way in which "inputs" are accepted: notice that the actual keyword INPUT is not used at all. The technique used for this is described at length in the "subroutines" section of this book ("A Matter of Routine"). The *reason* this technique has been adopted is that INPUT causes the computer to wait for the user to press ENTER before continuing with the program, which is clearly inappropriate in a case like this where a time limit for an entry is required.

The command OVER 1 is used in the program to erase the fuse, one pixel at a time, (line 500), and to erase incorrect entries (line 105).

NOTE: If at first you need a longer fuse, increase the value of t (line 25) to 15 or 20.

CHR TEST

```
10 BORDER 6: PAPER 7: INK 2: CLS
15 PRINT AT 15,5;"BOMB"
20 CIRCLE 56,52,39
25 LET t=10
30 PLOT 56,91: DRAW 0,5: DRAW t,t: PLOT OVER 1;
      56+t,96+t
35 LET x=INT (RND*223)+33
40 IF x>=144 AND x<=164 THEN GO TO 35
45 PRINT AT 0,0;"What is the code for:";CHR$ x
50 LET a$="": LET a=0
55 PAUSE 10: LET i$=INKEY$
60 GO SUB 500
65 IF t=0 THEN GO TO 950
70 IF i$=CHR$ 13 THEN GO TO 100
75 IF i$<"0" OR i$>"9" THEN GO TO 55
80 LET a$=a$+i$: LET a=VAL a$: PRINT AT 2,22;a$: GO TO 55
100 IF a=x THEN GO TO 900
105 PRINT AT 2,22; OVER 1;a$: GO TO 50
500 DRAW OVER 1;-1,-1
510 LET t=t-1: RETURN
900 PRINT AT 5,11; FLASH 1;"WELL DONE!!": GO TO 1000
950 FOR k=1 TO 2: FOR j=0 TO 7: PAPER j: BORDER j:
      CLS: BEEP .01,k*7-j: NEXT j: NEXT k: BORDER 6
1000 PRINT "The code for ";CHR$ x;" is: ";x
1010 PRINT AT 21,0;"Press ""R"" to Re-run"
1020 IF INKEY$="r" OR INKEY$="R" THEN RUN
1030 GO TO 1020
9000 SAVE "CHR TEST" LINE 0
```

ATTR TABLE

You probably realized from your earliest experiments with the Timex Sinclair that some of the combinations of INK and PAPER colors simply do not work. Anything printed in cyan INK on magenta PAPER, for example, will appear as an unreadable blur.

This program shows you exactly which combinations do work (surprisingly few of them), but it also serves a far more useful purpose. It tabulates the ATTRIBUTE number associated with each particular combination. (e.g., the aforementioned cyan INK/magenta PAPER combination has ATTR 29).

You will find this table indispensable when writing programs which use the ATTR function, or when POKEing values into the Attributes file.

Notice that by using the *Global* command BRIGHT 1 (line 10), and then printing everything using BRIGHT 0 (lines 30, 40 and 70), white characters, and even white PAPER, show up very clearly against a white background.

For BRIGHT characters, add 64 to the ATTR values shown, and for FLASHing characters, add 128.

```
ATTR TABLE

10 BRIGHT 1: CLS: PRINT TAB 15;" PAPER "''''''''''
        "I"''"N"''"K"
20 FOR j=0 TO 7
30 PRINT AT 2,j*3+6; PAPER j; BRIGHT 0;CHR$ 32;CHR$ 32
40 PRINT AT j*2+5,2; PAPER j; BRIGHT 0;CHR$ 32
50 FOR k=0 TO 7
60 LET a$=STR$ (8*j+k): IF LEN a$=1 THEN LET a$=CHR$ 32+a$
70 PRINT PAPER j; INK k; BRIGHT 0; AT k*2+5,j*3+6;a$
80 NEXT k
90 NEXT j
100 STOP
9000 SAVE "ATTR TABLE" LINE 0
```

PIANO

It is an easy matter to redefine the Timex Sinclair keyboard so that the keys produce different characters from those shown on them. You can even redefine it so that they do not produce characters at all, but musical notes.

This program redefines the top row of alpha keys (QWERTYUIOP) to produce the white notes of a piano (from middle C upwards: the easiest thing to remember is that key "E" produces note E), and the appropriately placed numeric keys to produce the black notes.

(If you look at a real piano keyboard, you will see that Timex Sinclair key "3" corresponds to D#, but key "4" does not correspond to any black note, and is therefore undefined).

The program works by producing a new character set in array a(). This is a very austere character set, consisting of no character at all for most keys, and the pitch values 1 to 17 for the keys shown in line 10. (The adjustments of +1 in lines 30 and 50 and –1 in line 60 are necessary because array elements begin at 1, whereas character codes begin at 0).

Line 60 rejects keypresses for which there is no corresponding tone-value, and produces half-second BEEP for the piano keys.

```
PIANO

10 LET n$="q2w3er5t6y7ui9o0p"
20 DIM a(256)
30 FOR j=1 TO 17: LET a(CODE n$(j)+1)=j
40 NEXT j
50 LET i=CODE INKEY$+1
60 IF a(i) THEN BEEP .5,a(i)-1
70 GO TO 50
9000 SAVE "PIANO" LINE 0
```

CLOCK

The following program produces a digital clock. Lines 10 to 70 convert hours and minutes entries into three values to be POKEd into the system variable FRAMES, and lines 100 to 140 perform the reverse operation, converting the value in FRAMES back into hours, minutes and seconds.

The remainder of the program merely arranges the output format for printing in line 180.

The program produces a 24-hour clock. If you are old fashioned enough to prefer the 12-hour variety, change statement 2 of line 140 to read:

```
IF h=13 THEN LET h=1
```

IMPORTANT NOTE

If you live in a country where the frequency is 50 hertz, replace "60" by "50" in line 30 and line 100.

```
CLOCK

1 BORDER 6: PAPER 6: INK 0: CLS
5 DIM t$(8): LET t$(3)=":": LET t$(6)=":"
10 INPUT "Hour ? ";h
20 INPUT "Minute ? ";m
30 LET a=(h*3600+m*60)*60
40 LET b=INT (a/65536): POKE 23674,b
50 LET c=a-b*65536
60 LET a=INT (c/256): POKE 23673,a
70 LET b=c-a*256: POKE 23672,b
100 LET t=INT ((65536*PEEK 23674+256*PEEK 23673+PEEK
        23672)/60)
110 LET h=INT (t/3600)
120 LET b=t-h*3600
130 LET m=INT (b/60)
140 LET s=b-m*60: IF h=24 THEN LET h=0
150 LET t$( TO 2)=STR$ h: IF LEN STR$ h=1 THEN
        LET t$( TO 2)="0"+STR$ h
160 LET t$(4 TO 5)=STR$ m: IF LEN STR$ m=1 THEN
        LET t$(4 TO 5)="0"+STR$ m
170 LET t$(7 TO )=STR$ s: IF LEN STR$ s=1 THEN
        LET t$(7 TO )="0"+STR$ s
180 PRINT AT 11,12;t$
190 GO TO 100
9000 SAVE "CLOCK" LINE 0
```

Q : What is wrong with this listing?

```
   5 CLEAR 29999
  10 LET C=PEEK 23606+256*PEEK 2
3607+256
  20 FOR J=0 TO 95
  30 FOR P=0 TO 7
  40 POKE 30000+7-P+8*J,PEEK (C+
P+8*J)
  50 NEXT P
  60 NEXT J
  70 POKE 23606,48: POKE 23607,1
16
  80 STOP
9000 SAVE "INVERT" LINE 0
9995 REM recovery
9996 POKE 23606,0: POKE 23607,60
```

A: Nothing at all. *To see how it is done, turn to page 74.*

2

Play It, Sam

- PRACTICE GAME
- SQUASH
- FORTRESS/FORT-DATA
- MINEFIELD

N.B. The Space Games are all in "PLAY IT AGAIN SAM."

PRACTICE GAME

Many people seem to think that they can walk into any video arcade, march straight up to the latest games machine, and immediately set up an unbeatable high score. The irritating thing, of course, is that many people can do precisely that. For the rest of us, practice may not make perfect, but it might at least enable us to avoid making complete fools of ourselves when faced with an arcade game.

This program simulates the most fundamental of all bat-and-ball type video games. There is no scoring, and no end to the game; you just have to keep trying to hit the balls which are launched at you constantly.

It is not as easy as it sounds, however. Because of the no frills approach, the game runs faster than most games written in Basic (although I have retained the sound-effects: if you want the game to run even faster you may eliminate these as well). Also, the conditions for hitting the ball are very severe. You must make a direct hit with the full face of the bat; edged shots are not allowed. (This rule is relaxed in the next program, "Squash", so once you have mastered the practice game, you should be ready to take on all comers at Squash).

The structure of the program is sufficient for you to develop it into any of the first generation type of video game (Breakout, etc.)

The ball coordinates (x,y) are modified by two variables: ud (up/down) and lr (left/right). Each of these may take either of the values –1 (up, left) or +1 (down, right). Hitting a side wall reverses the sign of lr; hitting the top wall or the bat reverses the sign of ud.

The bat coordinates (a, b, of which a is a constant) are modified by the INKEY$ routine in line 100.

In both cases, I have used the technique of printing a space where the bat/ball used to be. You can, of course, use OVER 1 to erase the old bat/ball if you prefer.

To enable the bat to move faster than the ball, it is merely necessary to call the bat movement subroutine twice for each movement of the ball (lines 30 and 45).

PRACTICE GAME

```
5 BORDER 4: PAPER 4: BRIGHT 1: INK 9
10 CLS
15 LET a=20: LET b=15: LET w=0
20 LET x=0: LET y=INT (RND*31): LET ud=1: LET lr=
        INT (RND*2): IF lr=0 THEN LET lr=-1
25 PRINT AT x,y;".": IF w THEN BEEP .01,30: LET w=0
30 GO SUB 100
35 LET nx=x+ud
40 IF nx=0 THEN LET ud=-ud: LET w=1
45 GO SUB 100
50 LET ny=y+lr: IF ny=0 OR ny=31 THEN LET lr=-lr: LET w=
55 IF nx=a AND ny=b THEN LET ud=-ud: BEEP .01,50
60 PRINT AT x,y;CHR$ 32: LET x=nx: LET y=ny
65 IF x=22 THEN BEEP .3,0: GO TO 20
70 GOTO 25
100 LET n=b+(INKEY$="8" AND b<31)-(INKEY$="5" AND b>0)
105 IF n<>b THEN PRINT AT a,b;CHR$ 32: LET b=n
110 PRINT AT a,b;CHR$ 95
115 RETURN
9000 SAVE "PRACTICE" LINE 0
```

SQUASH

Although it is clearly based on the previous program, this is a full fledged game for two players. (If you are anti-social, you may prefer playing your left hand against your right hand—very difficult.)

Obviously the main differences between "Squash" and "Practice Game" are in the bat movement routine. To allow two bats to be moved independently, the INKEY$ function is patently inadequate, as it fails to detect *any* keypress when two or more keys are depressed simultaneously. The IN function, however, though slightly more difficult to use, has the same effect, but can identify any number of keys being pressed together.

There are eight separate IN commands to read the whole keyboard; this program uses just two of them:

```
IN 63486 to read keys 1 to 5
IN 61438 to read keys 6 to 0
```

Keys 1 and 2 are used to move Player 1's bat left and right respectively, and keys 9 and 0 to move Player 2's bat. Lines 105 and 110 use the two IN commands in exactly the same way as INKEY$ (except that IN returns a NUMBER, whereas INKEY$ returns a STRING). The two IN commands *do not* interfere with each other in any way. IN 61438 returns a value of 253 whenever key "9" is pressed, and 254 whenever key "0" is pressed, regardless of any other keys being pressed on any other part of the keyboard. Similarly, IN 63486 returns 253 for key "2" and 254 for key"1". (Actually, the absolute values returned by IN depend on other factors besides keypresses, namely the status of the ear socket, which is affected by BEEP. Therefore line 35 ensures that the numbers returned will be in the correct range).

Changes to the ball movement section are less significant, and have been made to make the game rather more interesting than merely a two player version of "Practice".

Edged shots are now allowed (line 70), and cause the lr variable to be reversed. This makes the game much easier, effectively tripling the size of your bat, but it also gives scope for far more skill and ball-positioning.

To counteract this, the bat movement subroutine is only called ONCE for each ball movement. You *cannot* out-run the ball in this game, but remember that you *can* move your bat even when it is your opponent's shot. You cannot, of course, HIT your opponent's ball, as the bat coordinates are held in a two element array, and lines 75 and 80 look only at the appropriate bat when detecting a hit.

Scores are displayed on screen, and a score of 21 by either player wins the game.

SQUASH

```
5 BORDER 7: PAPER 6: INK 9: CLS
10 DIM s(2): DIM b(2): DIM n(2): LET w=0: LET b(1)=13:
        LET b(2)=17: LET s(1)=-1: LET p=0
15 LET x=0: LET y=INT (RND*31): LET ud=1: LET p=p+1:
        IF p=3 THEN LET p=1
20 LET lr=INT (RND*3)-1: IF NOT lr THEN GO TO 20
25 LET s(p)=s(p)+1
30 PRINT AT 21,0;"To play:";p;" SCORES: 1=";s(1);TAB 26;
        "2=";s(2): IF s(1)=21 OR s(2)=21 THEN GO TO 1000
35 OUT 63486,255: OUT 61438,255
40 PRINT AT x,y;".": IF w THEN BEEP .01,30: LET w=0
45 GO SUB 100
50 LET nx=x+ud
55 IF nx=0 THEN LET ud=-ud: LET w=1
60 LET ny=y+lr: IF ny=0 OR ny=31 THEN LET lr=-lr: LET w=1
65 IF ud=-1 OR nx<18 THEN GO TO 85
70 IF nx=17+p AND ABS (ny-b(p))=1 THEN LET ud=-ud: LET lr=
        ny-b(p): BEEP .01,50: LET p=p+1: IF p=3 THEN LET p=1
75 IF nx=17+p AND ny=b(p) THEN LET ud=-ud: BEEP .01,50:
        LET p=p+1: IF p=3 THEN LET p=1
80 PRINT AT 21,8;p
85 PRINT AT x,y;CHR$ 32: LET x=nx: LET y=ny
90 IF x=21 THEN BEEP .3,0: GO TO 15
95 GO TO 40
100 PRINT AT 18,b(1);CHR$ 95;AT 19,b(2);CHR$ 95
105 LET n(2)=b(2)+(IN 61438=254 AND b(2)<31)-(IN 61438=253
        AND b(2)>0)
110 LET n(1)=b(1)+(IN 63486=253 AND b(1)<31)-(IN 63486=254
        AND b(1)>0)
115 IF n(1)=b(1) THEN GO TO 125
120 PRINT AT 18,n(1);CHR$ 95;AT 18,b(1);CHR$ 32:
        LET b(1)=n(1)
125 IF n(2)=b(2) THEN RETURN
130 PRINT AT 19,n(2);CHR$ 95;AT 19,b(2);CHR$ 32:
        LET b(2)=n(2): RETURN
1000 PRINT AT 5,1; PAPER 7; FLASH 1;"GAME OVER : Press R
        for replay"
1005 IF INKEY$="r" THEN RUN
1010 GO TO 1005
9000 SAVE "SQUASH" LINE 0
```

FORTRESS/FORT-DATA

"Fortress" is more of an intellectual puzzle than a game in the conventional sense. It is very easy if you know the secret, and virtually impossible if you don't. The Timex Sinclair, of course, knows the secret, and so plays very well.

The two programs should be entered as follows:

> Key in "FORT-DATA"
>
> RUN. This will establish the arrays, but you will see nothing on screen, except for the STOP statement report.
>
> Enter CONT to save a copy of "FORT-DATA", together with its arrays, on tape
>
> Do *not* enter NEW
>
> Simply key in "FORTRESS", and allow the lines of "FORT-DATA" to be replaced by those of "FORTRESS"
>
> Do *not* enter RUN. Use GO TO 9000 to save a copy of "FORTRESS" and the arrays from "FORT-DATA". This copy will "auto run" when LOADed, without clearing the arrays. You may run the program immediately, not by entering RUN, but by using GO TO 0.

If you do accidentally enter RUN (or CLEAR) while keying in "FORTRESS", do not worry. Simply continue keying in the program, then:

> Enter GO TO 9000 to save
>
> Enter LOAD "FORT-DATA"
>
> Load "FORT-DATA" from tape, and it will "auto run," producing the STOP report as before
>
> Now enter MERGE "FORTRESS"
>
> Finally, enter GO TO 9000 to save another copy of "FORTRESS", this time with the arrays intact.

Why all this fuss? Why not just combine the programs into one?

The reason is *not* to save memory, although the technique does achieve this, and you should bear it in mind for when you write longer programs. The reason it is used here is more subtle: people are becoming so computer literate these days that traditional problem solving methods are being neglected. Faced with a quiz type program, many people would make no attempt to answer the questions conventionally, but would merely BREAK the program and search through the listing for the required answers. I have seen many commercial quiz programs where questions and answers are actually listed together in the same statement.

The moral of this is that it is no longer adequate to idiot-proof you programs; you must now genius-proof them as well.

In "Fortress", the solution is not actually explicit in the listing, but the key is contained by the numbers held in array ( ). By using this two-program technique, it is possible to refer to this array without revealing its contents in the listing.

Playing The Game

"Fortress" can be played by two players, or one player and the computer. The two players are known as the ATTACKER and the DEFENDER. The playing board represents a castle, with 18 rooms (marked A to R). Each room has four exits, each one leading to a passage to an adjacent room. (The plan of the castle is drawn on screen to make this clear). The object of both players is to try and capture their opponent by entering the same room as him.

There are different restrictions on the movements of the two players:

> The Defender may not leave the keep i.e., the triangle formed by rooms A, B and D.
>
> The Attacker may enter any room, but may not use any passage more than once. (Passages are deleted from the screen once they have been used). It is possible, therefore, for the Attacker to forfeit the game by becoming trapped in a room from which all four exits have been used. The Attacker *always* moves first.

On the face of it, then, the Defender has a rather boring role. He can only wander among the three rooms of the keep, waiting for the Attacker to come into range. Try playing a few games against a friend (let him be the Defender) and you will probably beat him easily. Pretty soon he will want to take over the role of Attacker, so let him, but let the computer take over the defense. I can *guarantee* that the computer will win.

The computer's defense at "Fortress" is infallible, and its attack, though beatable, is very good too. In order to win, you must play the Defender, and you must either have a lot of luck *or* adopt the same strategy which the computer uses in defense. I am not going to tell you exactly what that strategy is, but I have already told you where to find the key and the rest is up to you.

Program Notes

The arrays created by "Fort-data" are as follows:

p (18, 2): DATA line 1000: The PRINT AT coordinates of the 18 rooms of the castle

q (18, 2): The same screen positions, converted to PLOT coordinates. (Array p will be used to print the room letters, and also the player positions. Array q will be used in DRAWing the connecting passages)

c (18): DATA line 2000: work this one out for yourself.

1$ (18, 4): DATA line 3000: The "legal moves" from each room at the beginning of play. This array will later be copied into another array m$(18, 4), and as passages are used, elements of m$ are replaced with asterisks (CHR$ 42). 1$ remains unchanged ready for the next game.

"Fortress" itself begins (at line 100) by creating two User Defined Graphics: CHR$ 144 for the attacker and CHR$ 145 for the defender. The earlier lines comprise four subroutines for: printing the board (lines 5 to 50), printing an error message (60), printing the attacker (70) and printing the defender (75).

The four main sections of the program are:

1000 to 1240: Attacker move (Human entry)

2000 to 2140: Defender move (Human entry)

8000 to 8050: Defender move (Computer)

8500 to 8650: Attacker move (Computer)

The four lines 500 to 530 control the sequence in which these sections (only two of which are required for any one game) are called.

FORT-DATA

```
10 DIM p(18,2): DIM a(18,2)
20 RESTORE: FOR j=1 TO 18: READ p(j,1),p(j,2)
30 LET a(j,1)=4+p(j,2)*8: LET a(j,2)=172-p(j,1)*8
40 NEXT j
50 DIM c(18): FOR j=1 TO 18: READ c(j): NEXT j
60 DIM l$(18,4): FOR j=1 TO 18: READ l$(j): NEXT j
70 STOP
1000 DATA 1,12,1,18,3,6,3,15,3,24,5,10,5,20,7,8,7,22,9,6,9,
        24,11,9,11,21,13,13,13,17,14,8,14,22,16,15
2000 DATA 1,2,3,3,3,2,1,1,2,2,1,3,3,2,1,1,2,3
3000 DATA "BCDF","ADEG","AFHJ","ABFG","BGIK","ADCH","BDEI",
        "CFJL","GEKM","CHLP","EIMQ","HJPN","IKQO","LOPR",
        "MNQR","JLNR","MKOR","NOPQ"
9000 SAVE "FORT-DATA" LINE 0
```

FORTRESS

```
1 GOTO 100
5 CLS: FOR j=1 TO 18
10 FOR k=1 TO 4
15 PLOT INK 4;a(j,1),a(j,2)
20 IF l$(j,k)>CHR$ (j+64) THEN GO TO 35
25 DRAW INK 4;a(CODE l$(j,k)-64,1)-a(j,1),a(CODE l$(j,k)-64,2)
        -a(j,2)
30 NEXT k
35 NEXT j
40 FOR j=1 TO 18: PRINT AT p(j,1),p(j,2);CHR$ (j+64): NEXT j
50 RETURN
60 PRINT AT 21,0;e$: FOR j=1 TO 100: NEXT j: PRINT AT 21,0;
        OVER 1;e$: RETURN
70 PRINT INK 2; AT p(ap,1),p(ap,2);CHR$ 144: RETURN
75 PRINT INK 1; AT p(dp,1),p(dp,2);CHR$ 145: RETURN
100 RESTORE: FOR j=USR CHR$ 144 TO USR CHR$ 145+7:
        READ a: POKE j,a: NEXT j
150 BORDER 6: PAPER 6: BRIGHT 1: INK 9: CLS
160 DIM m$(18,4): FOR j=1 TO 18: LET m$(j)=l$(j): NEXT j
170 LET ap=18: LET dp=4
180 DIM e$(20)
190 LET w$="": LET g=0: RANDOMIZE
200 CLS: PRINT TAB 11;"FORTRESS";AT 5,0;"1: 1 Player game"''
        "2: 2 Player game"
210 LET i$=INKEY$: IF i$<"1" OR i$>"2" THEN GO TO 210
220 LET no=2: IF i$="1" THEN GO SUB 3000
230 GO SUB 5: GO SUB 70: GO SUB 75
500 IF no<>100 THEN GO TO 1000
510 GOTO 8500
520 IF no<>97 THEN GO TO 2000
530 GO TO 8000
1000 PRINT AT 21,0;"Attacker move ("; INK 2;CHR$ 144;
        INK 9;")"
1010 IF m$(ap)="****" THEN LET w$="DEFENDER": GO TO 7000
1020 LET i$=INKEY$
1030 IF i$<"a" OR i$>"r" THEN GO TO 1020
1040 LET e$="NO PASSAGE"
```

[continued]

```
1050 FOR j=1 TO 4
1060 IF m$(ap,j)=CHR$ (CODE i$-32) THEN GO TO 1100
1070 IF m$(ap,j)=CHR$ 42 AND l$(ap,j)=CHR$ (CODE i$-32) THEN
     LET e$="PASSAGE USED": LET j=4
1080 NEXT j
1090 GO SUB 60: GO TO 1000
1100 LET nap=CODE i$-96
1110 LET m$(ap,j)=CHR$ 42
1120 FOR j=1 TO 4
1130 IF m$(nap,j)=CHR$ (ap+64) THEN LET m$(nap,j)=CHR$ 42
1140 NEXT j
1150 IF nap=dp THEN LET w$="ATTACKER"
1160 LET x=ap: LET y=nap: IF nap>ap THEN LET x=nap: LET y=ap
1170 PLOT q(x,1),q(x,2)
1180 DRAW OVER 1; INK 4;q(y,1)-q(x,1),q(y,2)-q(x,2)
1190 PRINT AT p(ap,1),p(ap,2);CHR$ (ap+64)
1200 LET ap=nap
1210 GO SUB 70
1220 IF INKEY$=i$ THEN GO TO 1220
1230 IF w$="" THEN GO TO 520
1240 GO TO 7000
2000 PRINT AT 21,0;"Defender move ("; INK 1;CHR$ 145;
     INK 9;")"
2010 LET i$=INKEY$
2020 IF i$="" OR i$=CHR$ 13 THEN GO TO 2010
2030 IF i$="a" OR i$="b" OR i$="d" THEN GO TO 2070
2040 LET e$="STAY IN YOUR AREA"
2050 GO SUB 60
2060 GO TO 2000
2070 LET ndp=CODE i$-96
2080 IF ndp=dp THEN GO TO 2010
2090 IF ndp=ap THEN LET w$="DEFENDER"
2100 PRINT AT p(dp,1),p(dp,2);CHR$ (dp+64)
2110 LET dp=ndp: GO SUB 75
2120 IF INKEY$=i$ THEN GO TO 2120
2130 IF w$="" THEN GO TO 500
2140 GO TO 7000
3000 PRINT '"A: You will be the ATTACKER"''"D: You will be
     the DEFENDER"
3010 LET i$=INKEY$: IF i$<>"a" AND i$<>"d" THEN GO TO 3010
3020 LET no=CODE i$: RETURN
7000 IF w$(1)="D" AND no=100 THEN LET w$="YOU"
7010 IF no=97 OR (no=100 AND w$(1)="A") THEN LET w$="I"
7020 PRINT AT 21,0;w$;" WIN";: IF no=2 THEN PRINT "S";
7030 PRINT "             ": REM 13 spaces
7040 INPUT "P= Play again : S= Stop ";i$
7050 IF i$<>"p" AND i$<>"s" THEN GO TO 7040
7060 IF i$="s" THEN GO TO 9999
7070 GO TO 150
8000 LET i$=CHR$ (c(ap)+64+(c(ap)=3))
8010 PRINT AT 21,0;"MY MOVE ";i$;" (Press ENTER)"
8020 IF INKEY$<>CHR$ 13 THEN GO TO 8020
8030 PRINT AT 21,17;"      ": REM 6 spaces
8040 LET i$=CHR$ (CODE i$+32)
8050 GO TO 1050+(1020 AND no=97)
8500 LET g=g+1: IF g=1 THEN LET i$=m$(ap,INT (RND*4)+1):
     GO TO 8010
```

```
8510 DIM g(4): FOR j=1 TO 4
8520 LET pm=CODE m$(ap,j)-64
8530 IF pm=-22 THEN LET g(j)=-30: GO TO 8600
8540 IF c(pm)=c(dp) THEN LET g(j)=15: GO TO 8600
8550 IF pm=dp THEN LET g(j)=30: GO TO 8600
8560 IF pm<3 OR pm=4 THEN LET g(j)=-10: GO TO 8600
8570 FOR k=1 TO 4
8580 IF m$(pm,k)=CHR$ 42 THEN LET g(j)=g(j)-1
8590 NEXT k
8600 NEXT j
8610 LET k=g(1)
8620 FOR j=2 TO 4: IF g(j)>k THEN LET k=g(j)
8630 NEXT j
8640 IF k=-30 THEN LET w$="DEFENDER":  GO TO 7000
8650 FOR j=1 TO 4: IF g(j)<>k THEN NEXT j
8660 LET i$=m$(ap,j): GO TO 8010
9000 SAVE "FORTRESS" LINE 100
9500 DATA 60,60,60,126,255,255,60,60,102,255,255,126,
     60,60,24,24
9999 STOP
```

MINEFIELD

This is a deceptively simple game which does not demand quite the same intellectual dexterity as "Fortress," but nevertheless requires a certain amount of skill to win.

The object is to march each of your three men 27 paces across a minefield, using a simulated dice-throw to determine the number of paces to be taken each move. The mines are all *clearly marked* (in red INK; safe ground is marked in green), and apart from the two adjacent mines near the end, they are all evenly spaced. I told you it would sound simple.

Of course, luck plays its part, as in any dice game, but the skill lies in selecting the correct man to move to make the best use of the throw. Positional play is all important, both on the minefield itself, and in the end game position when you have one or more men beyond the last two mines.

Program Notes

Array a() is a two dimensional array, the first dimension holding the position of each of the three men and the second being a FLAG which is set when the man is dead.

Thus, attempting to move a dead man (a(m,2)=1), or a man who has arrived home (a(m,1)=28) is detected as an illegal move in line 150.

Line 190 also uses the second dimension of the array as a parameter of FLASH, so that for a live man, the character is printed using FLASH 0, and for a dead man, FLASH 1.

I have not used any User Defined Graphics in the program, so for "man" in the above, read "asterisk." There is plenty of scope for you to enhance the program with sound and graphics; realistic explosions, scenery etc.

MINEFIELD

```
10 BORDER 6: PAPER 6: INK 9: CLS
20 DIM c$(32): DIM a(3,2): FOR j=1 TO 3: LET a(j,1)=1:
       NEXT j
30 PRINT AT 4,1;: FOR j=1 TO 6: PRINT INK 4;"---";
       INK 2;"-";: NEXT j
40 PRINT INK 2;"-"; INK 4;"--"; INK 7;CHR$ 143
50 FOR j=1 TO 3: PRINT AT j,1;"*": NEXT j
60 RANDOMIZE
100 LET x=INT (RND*6)+1
110 PRINT AT 10,0;"MOVE ";x;" PACE";: IF x<>1 THEN PRINT "S"
120 PRINT AT 15,0;"Which Man (1-3)"
130 LET i$=INKEY$: IF i$<"1" OR i$>"3" THEN GOTO 130
140 LET m=VAL i$
150 IF a(m,2) OR a(m,1)=28 THEN GO TO 500
160 LET pn=a(m,1)+x
170 LET p=pn/4: IF pn<28 AND p=INT p OR pn=25 THEN LET
       a(m,2)=1
180 IF pn>28 THEN LET pn=28
190 PRINT AT m,a(m,1);CHR$ 32;TAB pn; FLASH a(m,2);"*"
200 LET a(m,1)=pn
210 LET w=0: LET d=0: FOR j=1 TO 3: IF a(j,2) THEN LET d=d+1
220 IF a(j,1)=28 THEN LET w=w+1
230 NEXT j
240 IF d=3 THEN PRINT AT 19,10; FLASH 1;"ALL MEN DEAD!":
       GO TO 700
250 IF w=3 THEN PRINT AT 19,10; FLASH 1; INK 2; PAPER 7;
       "CONGRATULATIONS": GO TO 700
255 LET d$=" MAN": IF d<>1 THEN LET d$(3)="E"
260 IF d+w=3 THEN PRINT AT 19,4; FLASH 1;"GAME OVER : ";
       d;d$;" KILLED!": GO TO 700
270 IF INKEY$=i$ THEN GOTO 270
280 GO TO 100
500 PRINT AT 20,10; FLASH 1;"INVALID MOVE": FOR j=1 TO 20:
       NEXT j
510 PRINT AT 20,0;c$: GO TO 130
700 PRINT AT 21,0;"Press P to play : X to stop"
710 IF INKEY$="p" THEN RUN
720 IF INKEY$="x" THEN STOP
730 GO TO 710
9000 SAVE "MINEFIELD" LINE 0
```

3

Not Just Your Plaything

- CALCULATOR
- WORD PROCESSOR
- INVOICING (48K)/SALES LEDGER (48K)
- BIORHYTHMS

CALCULATOR

This program will enable your Timex Sinclair to function almost as well as a cheap pocket calculator. The Timex Sinclair has many complex mathematical functions built in, as well as a very large number of memory locations, none of which are exploited in this program, so if you feel like developing it to make use of these, feel free to do so. Personally, I would rather use a pocket calculator.

Notes On Use

The program uses the same logic as most (cheap) pocket calculators. In other words, enter calculations just as you would write them on paper and the screen will display either your current entry (after you have pressed a numeric key) or the running total so far (after an arithmetic operator). You will also get an irritating BEEP with every key.

The only arithmetic operators the program will accept are +, –, *, / and =. You do not have to press SYMBOL SHIFT to obtain any of these or the decimal point (although it does not matter if you do). Also, as you probably use a computer more often than you use a calculator and may therefore associate the ENTER key with finality rather than the "equals" key, these two keys both have the same effect of displaying the total.

To correct erroneous entries, you may either use key "C" (described below) or DELETE, which works as normal. (Not many calculators allow you to delete entries in this way, but all computers do, and I expect that it is a feature you would not like to lose).

Key "C" acts as a dual function CLEAR (in the calculator sense, not the computer sense). UNSHIFTED it will act as a CLEAR ENTRY key, retaining the running total, and SHIFTED (using CAPS SHIFT) it will act as a CLEAR AND RESET key.

Overflow errors in your entries will be detected and signaled, but overflow errors during a calculation will of course crash the program with report code 6.

Line 2010 warrants some explanation. a$ is the current entry. If you press an arithmetic operator when there is no current entry, then the operation is performed on the current running total (r$). If there is no current running total, then the operation is performed on the previous grand total (q$). Only if there is no current entry, no running total and no previous grand total is the operation rejected. (Different pocket calculators use different logic in this respect, but mine is a very cheap model, and that is how mine works.)

CALCULATOR

```
10 CLS: PRINT TAB 10;"ZX Calculator"
100 LET r$=""
150 LET q$=""
200 LET s$="mkjbvl"+CHR$ 13
250 LET x$=".+-*/"+CHR$ 13+CHR$ 13
1000 LET a$="": LET j=0: LET d=0
1010 PAUSE 0: LET i$=INKEY$
1020 FOR k=1 TO 7
1030 IF i$=s$(k) OR i$=x$(k) THEN GO TO 2000
1040 NEXT k
1050 IF i$="c" OR i$="C" THEN GO TO 5020
1060 IF i$=CHR$ 12 AND j<>0 THEN LET j=j-1: LET a$=a$
        ( TO j): GO TO 1100
1070 IF i$<"0" OR i$>"9" THEN GO TO 1010
1080 IF j=31 THEN GO TO 5000
1090 LET a$=a$+i$: LET j=j+1
1100 GO SUB 4000: PRINT a$: BEEP .01,30
1110 GO TO 1010
2000 LET i$=x$(k): IF i$="." THEN GO TO 3000
2005 IF a$="." THEN GO TO 1010
2010 IF a$="" THEN LET a$=r$: IF a$="" THEN LET a$=q$:
        IF a$="" THEN GO TO 1000
2020 IF r$="" THEN LET r$=a$: LET b$=i$: PRINT AT 12,31;b$:
        BEEP .01,50: GO TO 1000
2030 LET r$=STR$ (VAL (r$+b$+a$))
2040 LET j=LEN r$: GO SUB 4000: PRINT r$: BEEP .05,40
2050 LET b$=i$: IF i$=CHR$ 13 THEN LET b$=CHR$ 32:
        LET q$=r$: LET r$=""
2060 PRINT AT 12,31;b$: IF b$<> CHR$ 32 THEN BEEP .01,50
2070 GOTO 1000
3000 IF d THEN GO TO 1010
3010 LET d=1: GO TO 1090
4000 DIM c$(32-j): PRINT AT 11,0;c$;: RETURN
5000 PRINT AT 15,14; FLASH 1;"ERROR"
5005 LET i$=INKEY$
5010 IF i$<>"c" AND i$<>"C" THEN GO TO 5005
5015 PRINT AT 15,14;"     "
5020 DIM c$(32): PRINT AT 11,0;c$
5025 IF i$="C" THEN GO TO 100
5030 GO TO 1000
9000 SAVE "CALC" LINE 0
```

WORD PROCESSOR

If your Timex Sinclair is interfaced to a letter-quality printer for output and T/S disc drives for storage, then you may well find that this program does not meet all your requirements of a word processor. If, however, you have a minimal hardware configuration of 16K Timex Sinclair, T/S Printer and cassette recorder, it should be more than adequate.

It provides the standard features of a word processor: Input and Edit facilities (albeit somewhat limited, see below), tape storage and recall, optional right justification (i.e., alignment of the right hand margin), etc.

The program will hold up to five screen-pages of text (20 lines each), i.e., 100 lines in total. If you have more than 16K RAM, this can be increased dramatically by redimensioning w$ in line 5 and also making the appropriate changes to lines 1200 and 7030. (See Program Notes.)

Notes On Use

INPUT (FROM KEYBOARD)

On running, select option "K" to enter text from the keyboard. A flashing cursor will appear in the current print position, i.e. the top left hand corner. Enter text as you would with a typewriter, and as you reach column 25 a BEEP will sound signifying the approaching end of line. You may continue typing, and a space or hyphen will automatically bring the cursor onto the next line. If you do not use a space or hyphen before column 32, a hyphen will be inserted automatically. (Sometimes this is desirable and sometimes it is not. You may prefer to go back and either delete the entire word, or reposition the hyphen somewhere else. Both options are possible: see EDITING.)

If you wish to start a new paragraph, the ENTER key will also move the cursor to the start of the next line. (Press ENTER twice if you like to leave a blank line between paragraphs). You may indent the new paragraph by one space or more, but if you require the final text to be right justified, use *one space only*.

If you do not have 20 lines of text to enter, press "." when the cursor is against the left hand margin (i.e., start a new line with a full stop).

When you do this, or when you have completed 20 lines of text, the message:

```
P= PRINT :J= JUSTIFY :C= CONT
```

will appear. These options work as follows:

PRINT: Produces an identical copy of your text on the T/S Printer. Returns to the same three option message, so you may produce as many copies as you require.

JUSTIFY: Justifies your text ON THE SCREEN. Also reformats the text in the computer's memory, so once justified, text cannot be unjustified. Returns to the same three option message, so you may either PRINT the justified text, or proceed without printing.

CONT: Gives a further option to either enter more text, or save your completed text on tape.

EDITING

There is no separate edit mode as on some word processors. You may edit the text as you are compiling it (and at no other time). Always ensure that editing is complete before the end of each page is reached, as you will have no opportunity to go back at that stage. Use the DELETE key as normal to erase mistakes spotted immediately; otherwise use the cursor left key (CAPS SHIFT "5") to position the cursor at the required place, then simply type over the text to be amended. Use the cursor right key (CAPS SHIFT "8") to return the cursor to the current text position.

IMPORTANT NOTE

When you have been amending a line at the top of the screen, you may be tempted to use the ENTER key to return the cursor to the bottom much more rapidly than by using CAPS SHIFT "8". However, remember that, if you select the JUSTIFY option, lines of text which have been terminated automatically by the computer will be justified. Lines which have been terminated by your pressing ENTER (normally end of paragraph or end of text lines) will not. Therefore, by using this method of cursor movement, effectively you will be telling the computer that none of these lines are to be justified.

SAVE ON TAPE

Entry to this mode has already been explained above. You will be asked to give a filename to your text, and the computer will confirm that it is indeed being saved under this filename. (The Timex Sinclair will not allow filenames of more than 10 characters; so if you do enter a longer name, this will be truncated, and the name shown on screen will be the actual name under which your text is saved, and by which it should later be recalled.) Saving your text terminates the program. You may verify the operation by entering:

```
VERIFY n$ DATA w$()
```

If the tape fails to verify, or if you require a back-up copy for any reason, enter:

```
GO TO 8030
```

RECALL FROM TAPE

Run the program and press "T". You will be asked for the appropriate filename, and the text will be loaded and printed *direct to the T/S printer*. It will be printed one page at a time, so you have the option to repeat pages, or continue until the text is complete, at which point you may repeat some or all of the text, or terminate the program.

Program Notes

If you want to add any further features to this word processor, the main sections of the program are:

300 to 600 : INPUT (lines 320 to 400= control characters)

1000 to 1210 : PRINT option and various sub-menus

5000 to 5300 : Justification

7000 to 7070 : LOAD from tape

8000 to 8050 : SAVE on tape

The variable *x* is used to indicate the page number (assuming the first page to be numbered 0), so if you increase the maximum file size, *x* should be allowed to reach, but not exceed, the new maximum (lines 1200 and 7030).

The current line of the current page is indicated by j; l is the current column position and w$ is the actual text file. So the expression:

```
w$(x*20+j+1,l)
```

which occurs several times in the program identifies precisely the correct element of w$ corresponding to the cursor position.

```
WORD PROCESSOR

5 DIM w$(100,32): DIM b$(32)
10 CLS: PRINT TAB 10;"ZX WORDPRO";AT 5,0;"T = LOAD TEXT FROM
       TAPE"''"K = ENTER TEXT FROM KEYBOARD"
15 IF INKEY$="k" OR INKEY$="K" THEN GO TO 100
20 IF INKEY$="t" OR INKEY$="T" THEN GO TO 7000
25 GO TO 15
100 LET x=0
150 CLS
200 FOR j=0 TO 19
210 FOR l=0 TO 31
300 PRINT AT j,l; FLASH 1; OVER 1;CHR$ 32
310 PAUSE 0: LET i$=INKEY$
320 IF i$=CHR$ 8 AND l<>0 THEN LET l=l-2: GO TO 500
330 IF i$=CHR$ 8 AND j<>0 THEN PRINT AT j,0;w$(x*20+j+1,1):
       LET j=j-1: LET l=30: GO TO 500
340 IF i$=CHR$ 9 AND l<>31 THEN GO TO 500
350 IF i$=CHR$ 9 AND j<>19 THEN PRINT AT j,31; CHR$ (CODE
       (w$(x*20+j+1,32))+19*(w$(x*20+j+1,32)=CHR$ 13)):
       LET j=j+1: LET l=1: GO TO 500
360 IF l=0  AND i$="." THEN LET l=31: LET j=19: GO TO 540
370 IF i$=CHR$ 12 AND l<>0 THEN LET w$(x*20+j+1, l)=CHR$ 32:
       LET l=l-2: GO TO 500
380 IF i$=CHR$ 12 AND j<>0 THEN PRINT AT j,0;w$(x*20+j+1,1):
       LET j=j-1: LET l=31: LET w$(x*20+j+1, l)=CHR$ 32:
       LET l=l-2: GO TO 500
390 IF i$=CHR$ 13 THEN LET l=31: GO TO 410
400 IF i$<CHR$ 32 THEN GO TO 310
410 IF l=31 AND i$<>CHR$ 32 AND i$<>CHR$ 13 THEN
       LET i$=CHR$ 45
420 BEEP .01,20+20*(i$=CHR$ 32)
430 LET w$(x*20+j+1, l+1)=i$
500 PRINT AT j,0;w$(x*20+j+1)
510 IF w$(x*20+j+1,32)=CHR$ 13 THEN PRINT AT j,31;CHR$ 32
520 IF l=26 THEN BEEP .5,50
530 IF l>25 AND (i$=CHR$ 32 OR i$=CHR$ 45) THEN LET l=32
540 NEXT l:  BEEP .5,20
600 NEXT j
1000 PRINT AT 21,0;"P= PRINT :J= JUSTIFY :C= CONT"
1010 IF INKEY$="C" OR INKEW$="c" THEN GO TO 1100
1020 IF INKEY$="P" OR INKEY$="p" THEN GO TO 1050
```

[continued]

```
1030 IF INKEY$="J" OR INKEY$="j" THEN GO SUB 5000: GO TO 1000
1040 GO TO 1010
1050 PRINT AT 21,0;b$: COPY: GO TO 1000
1100 CLS: PRINT "M= More Text :S= Save"
1110 IF INKEY$="M" OR INKEY$="m" THEN GO TO 1200
1120 IF INKEY$="S" OR INKEY$="s" THEN GO TO 8000
1130 GO TO 1110
1200 IF x=4 THEN PRINT AT 21,0;"No more room: Choose
      Save option": PAUSE 0: GO TO 1100
1210 LET x=x+1: GO TO 150
5000 PRINT AT 21,0;b$
5005 FOR j=x*20+1 TO x*20+20
5010 LET a$=w$(j)
5015 IF a$(32)<>CHR$ 32 THEN GO TO 5200
5020 LET s=0: FOR l=32 TO 1 STEP -1
5025 IF a$(l)<>CHR$ 32 THEN GO TO 5035
5030 LET s=s+1: NEXT l: IF s=32 THEN GO TO 5200
5035 LET d=2
5040 FOR l=2 TO 32
5045 IF a$(l)<>CHR$ 32 THEN GO TO 5090
5050 FOR k=32 TO l+1 STEP -1: LET a$(k)=a$(k-1): NEXT k
5055 LET l=l+d
5060 IF a$(32)<>CHR$ 32 THEN GO TO 5100
5090 NEXT l
5100 PRINT AT j-x*20-1,0;a$
5150 IF a$(32)=CHR$ 32 THEN LET d=d+1: GO TO 5040
5170 LET w$(j)=a$
5200 NEXT j
5300 RETURN
7000 INPUT "Filename ? ";n$
7005 IF n$="" THEN GO TO 7000
7010 PRINT AT 15,0;"LOAD TAPE ";n$
7015 LOAD n$ DATA w$()
7020 LET x=0
7025 FOR j=x+1 TO x+20: LPRINT w$(j): NEXT j
7030 LET x=x+20: IF x=100 THEN GO TO 7055
7035 CLS: PRINT "Press S to Stop"''"or any other
      key to continue"
7040 PAUSE 0
7045 IF INKEY$="s" OR INKEY$="S" THEN GO TO 7055
7050 GO TO 7025
7055 CLS: PRINT "TEXT COMPLETE"''"PRESS R TO REPEAT"''
      "OR X TO STOP "
7060 IF INKEY$="R" OR INKEY$="r" THEN GO TO 7020
7065 IF INKEY$="X" OR INKEY$="x" THEN GO TO 9999
7070 GO TO 7060
8000 INPUT "Filename ? ";n$
8010 IF n$="" THEN GO TO 8000
8020 IF LEN n$>10 THEN LET n$=n$( TO 10)
8030 PRINT "Saving as: ";n$
8040 SAVE n$ DATA w$()
8050 GO TO 9999
9000 CLEAR: SAVE "WP" LINE 0
9999 STOP
```

INVOICING (48K)/SALES LEDGER (48K)

If you run your own business then you certainly do not need me to tell you how tremendously useful a computer can be, particularly for such tasks as keeping your accounts.

If you do not run your own business, then you will probably be tempted to skip these next two programs, or even jump straight to the next games section. But hold on a second. Have you ever written a program and sold copies to your friends, or submitted a listing to one of the computer magazines? It could be that you are already in business as a software producer, and if you want to avoid an unpleasant confrontation with the taxman, you had better start keeping adequate records of all your transactions.

These two programs together form the "sales" side of what is usually referred to as an accountancy "suite" i.e., several programs which all serve independent functions, but which interact together, using the same data, to provide a complete set of accounts.

Invoicing provides an actual invoice for you to give to your customers, and also records every transaction in a sales daybook. Very simply, this is a list of all your sales, consisting of the date, customer's name, and amount. The total of the sales daybook should, therefore, represent your total business income for the particular period.

Of course, unless all your sales are on a strictly cash basis, the fact that you have issued certain invoices does not necessarily mean that all those customers will actually pay you, either correctly or on time. Keeping track of debtors is one of the most important parts of any business, and you do not have to be the size of a multinational corporation before the whole thing gets out of hand. That is where the sales ledger comes in.

This program uses the sales day book data (as compiled by Invoicing and referred to as INVOICES by both programs) to list each individual customer's account. All invoices issued are shown in one column, all payments made in another. If further payments have been received you may enter them on the appropriate ledger card. (Ledger card is a precomputer term, still in common use, meaning a particular account record.) The totals of invoices, payments, and outstanding balance will then be shown. You may make *hard copies* of ledger cards if you wish, either for your own information, or for use as statements to send to the customer.

Notes On Use

INVOICING

When you LOAD the program, the first thing to appear will be a three-option menu (see line 110). Taking each of these options in turn:

1. Produce Invoice: This will provide a list of all your customers to date, with a code number alongside each one. At the end of the list, with code number 0, will be the words "NEW CUSTOMER". (Naturally, the first time you run the program, this will be the *only* item on the list.) If you have had a lot of customers, you may have to use the Timex Sinclair's scrolling facility to reach the end of the list.

Enter the required customer code number. Numbers out of range will not be accepted. If you enter "0" then you will be asked to enter the customer's address (four lines in total; address line 1 should of course be the customer's name or the name of his or her business).

The invoice is then compiled on screen. Standard items, such as your address, are printed automatically; you merely have to enter:

a) The date
b) The narrative (i.e., what goods or services the invoice is for. Be succinct as no more than 22 characters of any narrative will be printed.)
c) The amount.

If there is more than one item to put on the invoice, you may add more narratives/amounts (but do not add too many, or the top of the invoice will scroll off screen, before the invoice is totaled).

You may then either copy the invoice to the T/S Printer, or cancel it if you have made an error.

2. List Invoices: You do not have to do anything when you select this option. The computer will produce the sales daybook listing (direct to the T/S Printer).

3. Save: You do not need to select this option after every invoice, or select it at all if you have not produced any invoices this run. You must, however, select it at the end of every run in which you have produced invoices.

There are two items to save:

- **a)** The invoice list/sales daybook saved as a character array under the filename "INVOICES"
- **b)** An up-dated copy of the program itself, ready for the next run.

NOTE: Options 1 and 2 return to the main menu after completion. Option 3 terminates the program. To reenter the program after termination or after a BREAK, use GO TO 100 (NOT RUN).

INVOICING

```
10 DIM a$(100,4,20)
20 LET nc=0: LET in=0
30 DIM b$(32)
40 DIM c$(100,3,10)
100 BORDER 6: PAPER 6: INK 9: CLS
110 PRINT AT 5,0;"1: Produce Invoice"'''"2: List
       Invoices"'''"3: SAVE "
120 LET i$=INKEY$: IF i$<"1" OR i$>"3" THEN GO TO 120
130 GO TO VAL i$*1000
500 DATA "V&H COMPUTER SERVICES"
510 DATA "182c KINGSTON RD."
520 DATA "STAINES"
530 DATA "MIDDLESEX"
1000 BORDER 5: PAPER 5: CLS
1010 FOR j=1 TO nc
1020 PRINT j;TAB 4;a$(j,1)
1030 NEXT j
1040 PRINT 0;TAB 4;"NEW CUSTOMER"
1050 INPUT "Customer number? ";t
1060 IF t<0 OR t>nc OR t<>INT t THEN GO TO 1050
1070 IF t<>0 THEN GO TO 1100
1080 LET nc=nc+1: FOR j=1 TO 4: INPUT AT j*2,0;("Address
       line ";j);":";a$(nc,j): NEXT j
1090 LET t=nc
1100 LET in=in+1
1110 CLS: RESTORE: FOR j=0 TO 3: READ t$: PRINT AT
       j,(32-LEN t$)/2;t$: NEXT j: PRINT: PRINT "INVOICE
       No.";in: PRINT
1120 INPUT "Date ";t$: LET c$(in,1)=t$:
       LET c$(in,2)=a$(t,1)
1130 PRINT TAB 31-LEN t$;t$
1140 FOR j=1 TO 4: PRINT a$(t,j): NEXT j: PRINT'':
       LET ip=0
1150 INPUT "Narrative ";t$: IF LEN t$>22 THEN LET
       t$=t$( TO 22)
1160 PRINT t$;
1170 INPUT "Price ";p: GO SUB 5000: IF x THEN GO TO 1170
1180 PRINT TAB 23;m$: LET ip=ip+p
1190 INPUT "Any more items (Y/N)? ";t$
1200 IF t$="y" OR t$="Y" THEN GO TO 1150
1210 IF t$="n" OR t$="N" THEN GO TO 1230
1220 GO TO 1190
```

[continued]

```
1230 PRINT AT 20,0;"TOTAL";: LET p=ip: GO SUB 5000
1240 PRINT TAB 23;m$
1250 PRINT AT 21,0;"C= COPY :X= CANC."
1260 IF INKEY$="c" OR INKEY$="C" THEN PRINT AT 21,0;b$:
        COPY : LET c$(in,3)=m$: GO TO 100
1270 IF INKEY$="x" OR INKEY$="X" THEN GO TO 1110
1280 GO TO 1260
2000 CLS: LET p=0: FOR j=1 TO in
2010 FOR k=1 TO 3
2020 LPRINT c$(j,k);
2030 NEXT k: LPRINT: LET p=p+VAL c$(j,3)
2040 NEXT j
2050 LPRINT : LPRINT "TOTAL";TAB 20;
2060 GO SUB 5000: LPRINT m$
2070 GO TO 100
3000 BORDER 4: PAPER 4: CLS
3010 PRINT "First SAVE invoice list for"''"SALES
        LEDGER program"
3020 SAVE "INVOICES" DATA c$()
3030 CLS: PRINT "Now SAVE entire program"''"(For use
        as INVOICING program"''"next time)"
3040 SAVE "INVOICING" LINE 100
3050 GO TO 9999
5000 REM insert "CASH" subroutine (see text)
9000 CLEAR : SAVE "INVOICING" LINE 0
```

SALES LEDGER

This program is SEQUENTIAL rather than MENU DRIVEN. Simply follow the instructions as they appear.

First load the latest INVOICES tape. The first ledger card will then be printed on screen. The first time you run the program the PAYMENTS column will of course be empty.

You will be asked if you wish to post (i.e. enter; more precomputer terminology) a payment. If you do, you must enter the date (of payment) and the amount, and the question will be repeated, allowing you to post further payments if necessary. When you have finished, the account is totaled, and you may either copy the ledger card to the T/S Printer, or proceed to the next account.

At the end of the run, the total outstanding (all accounts) will be displayed and you will be asked to save an up-dated copy of the program for next time. (Not strictly necessary if you have not posted any new payments, but a good habit to get into nevertheless, as very often by the end of a run you may have forgotten whether you have posted any payments or not.)

IMPORTANT NOTE

Always use the latest copy of each program when you begin a run. The master program itself contains no data, but every time you SAVE a copy, the current data is saved along with the program.

```
SALES LEDGER

10 DIM p$(100,3,10)
20 LET np=0
30 DIM b$(32)
40 LET tos=0
100 BORDER 6: PAPER 6: INK 9: CLS
110 PRINT "Please LOAD your INVOICES tape"
120 LOAD "INVOICES" DATA c$()
500 FOR a=1 TO 100: CLS
510 LET a$=c$(a,2)
520 LET c$(a,2)="x"
530 IF a$=b$( TO 10) THEN LET a=100: GO TO 990
540 IF a$="x"+b$( TO 9) THEN GO TO 990
550 PRINT TAB 12;a$
560 PRINT "DATE";TAB 10;"INVOICES";TAB 20;"PAYMENTS"
570 LET t=VAL c$(a,3)
580 PRINT c$(a,1);c$(a,3)
590 FOR k=1 TO 100
```

[continued]

```
600 IF c$(k,2)<>a$ THEN GO TO 640
610 LET t=t+VAL c$(k,3)
620 PRINT c$(k,1);c$(k,3)
630 LET c$(k,2)="x"
640 IF c$(k,2)="x"+b$( TO 9) THEN GO TO 660
650 IF c$(k,2)=b$( TO 10) THEN LET k=100
660 NEXT k
670 LET t1=0
700 FOR k=1 TO np
710 IF p$(k,2)<>a$ THEN GO TO 740
720 LET t1=t1+VAL p$(k,3)
730 PRINT p$(k,1);TAB 20;p$(k,3)
740 NEXT k
750 INPUT "POST A PAYMENT (Y/N)? ";t$
760 IF t$="n" OR t$="N" THEN GO TO 850
770 IF t$="y" OR t$="Y" THEN GO TO 790
780 GO TO 750
790 LET np=np+1: INPUT "Date ";p$(np,1): PRINT p$(np,1);
800 INPUT "Amount ";p: GO SUB 5000: IF x THEN GO TO 800
810 PRINT TAB 20;m$: LET p$(np,3)=m$: LET p$(np,2)=a$
820 LET t1=t1+VAL m$
830 GO TO 750
850 PRINT "TOTAL";TAB 10;
860 LET p=t: GO SUB 5000
870 PRINT m$;TAB 20;
880 LET p=t1: GO SUB 5000
890 PRINT m$
900 LET p=((INT (t*100)+.1)-(INT (t1*100)+.1))/100:
       GO SUB 5000
910 PRINT "O/S";TAB 10;m$: LET tos=tos+VAL m$
920 PRINT AT 21,0;"C= COPY :N= NEXT "
930 IF INKEY$="c" OR INKEY$="C" THEN PRINT AT 21,0;b$:
       COPY: GO TO 920
940 IF INKEY$="n" OR INKEY$="N" THEN GO TO 990
950 GO TO 930
990 NEXT a
1000 BORDER 4: PAPER 4: CLS
1010 LET p=tos: GO SUB 5000
1020 PRINT "TOTAL OUTSTANDING: ";m$'''
1030 PRINT "Now SAVE for use as SALES"''"program
       next time"
1040 SAVE "SALES" LINE 30: GO TO 9999
5000 REM insert "CASH" subroutine (see text)
9000 CLEAR : SAVE "SALES" LINE 0
```

Program Notes

The first thing to notice about both programs is that neither of the listings include the very important subroutine at line 5000. Do not worry, you do not have to pay extra for this. It is just such an incredibly useful subroutine which will probably become part of all your financial programs that it has been listed separately on page 00.

If, like normal readers, you started this book at the back, you may already have a copy of CASH on tape, in which case simply MERGE it into both these programs. Otherwise, SAVE what you have entered so far, enter NEW, key in CASH, SAVE it, and then MERGE in your current program. Do not merely key in the subroutine at the end of each program, as this will mean a lot of extra typing, and you still will not have a separate copy of CASH for future use.

The most likely problem you may encounter with these programs is that the TV screen may be just too small for the amount of information you need to display. Invoices with more than 6 lines of narrative, or ledger cards with more than 18 transactions, for instance. For most very small businesses, this will not occur, but if it does happen in your case, the easiest remedy is to dispense with the TV display completely, except for option prompts and INPUT lines. Change all other PRINT statements to LPRINT, and compile invoices/ledger cards directly onto the printer. (Delete the COPY instructions.)

The principal data arrays used are as follows:

a$ (100,4,20) :	Name and address file : INVOICING only
p$ (100,3,10) :	Payments : SALES LEDGER only
c$ (100,3,10) :	Invoices : Both programs

The three elements of both p$ and c$ (second dimension) are:

c$ (j,1) :	date
c$ (j,2) :	copy of address line 1 (name) from customer file
c$ (j,3) :	amount

IN is a VARIABLE NAME (for invoice number), and should not be confused with the Timex Sinclair keyword IN.

The DATA lines (500 to 530 of INVOICING) should, of course, contain your own name and address.

BIORHYTHMS

What, you may ask, is "Biorhythms" doing in the "Serious Applications" section, alongside such undeniably serious programs as "Invoicing" and "Sales Ledger"?

I will leave aside the controversial question of whether the *study* of biorhythms is, in itself, a serious business or just a harmless bit of fun. Suffice it to say that *serious* application does not necessarily mean *business* application, and there is a whole spectrum of uses to which you can put your computer. It does not have to be "*either* accountancy *or* games."

This program will plot three separate biocharts (Physical, Emotional and Intellectual cycles) for a period of about four months from any date you choose.

The actual plotting routine is confined to the three lines 220 to 240. All the rest is concerned with such mundane matters as:

User INPUT : lines 30 to 90

Drawing the graph baselines : line 210

Inserting the baseline scale : lines 300 to 330: Each mark on the baseline represents the first of the month; hence the slightly uneven calibration of the scale.

INPUT verification : lines 1000 to 1100 (no less than eleven lines to ensure that you have entered a valid date). This routine may be lifted piecemeal for use in other programs: for instance, both "Invoicing" and "Sales Ledger" allowed you to enter absolutely anything in response to the "Date ?" prompt. You might like to add this date verification routine to those or to other programs of your own.

Calculation of the number of days between your entered date and some hypothetical base date (year zero):
Lines 1500 to 1550 : The actual base date is unimportant as the program merely has to calculate the number of days between the two dates you enter.

BIORHYTHMS

```
10 BORDER 6: PAPER 6: INK 9: BRIGHT 1: CLS
20 LET m$="303232332323"
30 PRINT TAB 11;"BIORHYTHM"''''''"Please enter dates in
       the form:"'''TAB 11;"DD.MM.YY"
40 INPUT "Enter your date of birth ";d$
50 GO SUB 1000: IF x THEN GO TO 40
60 LET b=n: LET b$=d$
70 INPUT "Enter TODAY's date ";d$
80 GO SUB 1000: IF x THEN GO TO 70
90 LET n=n-b: IF n<0 THEN GO SUB 2000: GO TO 70
100 DIM n$(3,12): LET n$(1)="Physical": LET n$(2)=
       "Emotional": LET n$(3)="Intellectual"
110 DIM b(3): DIM c(3)
120 FOR j=1 TO 3
130 LET b(j)=18+5*j
140 LET c(j)=n-b(j)*INT (n/b(j))
150 NEXT j
200 CLS: PRINT TAB 11;"BIOCHART"''"D.O.B.:";b$,"Today:";d$
210 FOR j=1 TO 3: PLOT 0,j*48-28: DRAW 255,0: PRINT INK j;
       AT j*6-2,2;n$(j): NEXT j
220 FOR j=1 TO 3: FOR k=0 TO 255
230 PLOT INK j;k,SIN ((k+(2*c(j)))*PI/b(j))*20+((4-j)*48-28)
240 NEXT k: NEXT j
300 FOR j=0 TO 255
310 LET d=d+.5
320 IF d>CODE m$(m)-20 THEN LET d=.5: FOR k=1 TO 3:
       PLOT j,k*48-30: DRAW 0,5: NEXT k: LET m=m+1:
       IF m>12 THEN LET m=1
330 NEXT j
340 STOP
1000 LET x=0: PRINT AT 15,10;"            ": REM 12 spaces
1010 IF LEN d$<>8 THEN GO TO 2000
1020 IF d$(3)<>"." OR d$(6)<>"." THEN GO TO 2000
1030 FOR j=1 TO 7 STEP 3
1040 IF d$(j)<"0" OR d$(j)>"9" OR d$(j+1)<"0" OR d$(j+1)>"9"
       THEN GO TO 2000
1050 NEXT j
1060 LET y=VAL d$(7 TO ): LET m=VAL d$(4 TO 5): LET d=VAL
       d$( TO 2)
1070 IF y=0 OR d=0 OR m=0 OR m>12 THEN GO TO 2000
1080 LET l=0: IF y/4=INT y/4 THEN LET l=1
1090 LET n=CODE m$(m)-20+(m=2 AND l=1)
1100 IF d>n THEN GO TO 2000
1500 LET n=0
1510 FOR j=1 TO m-1
1520 LET n=n+CODE m$(j)-20
1530 NEXT j
1540 IF l=1 AND n>59 THEN LET n=n+1
1550 LET n=n+d+INT (365.25*(y-1)): RETURN
2000 LET x=1
2010 PRINT INK 2; FLASH 1; AT 15,10;"INVALID DATE": RETURN
9000 SAVE"BIORHYTHMS" LINE 0
```

4

Down Memory Lane

- DOWN MEMORY LANE
- READER 1
- READER 2
- TRACE
- RENUMBER
- CASE SWAP
- VARS

DOWN MEMORY LANE

The purpose of the programs in this section is to investigate part of the RAM area of the Timex Sinclair's memory.

You will see from the Timex Sinclair manual that the RAM is far from empty, even when the computer is first switched on. If you have a 16K Timex Sinclair then you might be shocked to discover that some 6K are occupied by the Display File, and another 1K by the Attributes File and System Variables, leaving only 9K of user memory for your programs.

However, the area of RAM on which I am going to concentrate *is* empty at switch on, and is the area between PROG and E-LINE, i.e. the area in which your program and variables will eventually be stored.

To find the boundaries of this area, enter the following three lines as COMMANDS (not as a program):

To find PROG, the address of the start of the program area:

```
PRINT PEEK 23635+256*PEEK 23636
```

To find VARS, the address of the boundary between the program and its variables:

```
PRINT PEEK 23627+256*PEEK 23628
```

To find E-LINE, the address of the end of the variable area:

```
PRINT PEEK 23641+256*PEEK 23642
```

You will find that the first two commands give the same result, and that the third gives a result just one higher (as the variable area always contains a byte CHR$ 118 (80h) to signify its end).

This means that the program, and its variables, occupy a total of one byte between them, which is hardly surprising as you have not got a program entered at this stage.

Now enter the same three lines, this time as a program (i.e., give them line numbers, say 10, 20 and 30), and then RUN.

This time, PROG will remain the same, but VARS and E-LINE will each have increased by 123 bytes, meaning that your short, three line program is occupying 123 bytes of RAM. E-LINE will still be only one byte above VARS, as your program has not used any variables.

Finally, edit the three program lines, replacing PRINT by LET a=, LET b=, and LET c=, and add a fourth line:

```
40 PRINT a'b'c
```

This will increase the program length to 140 bytes, and also the variable area to 13 bytes.

Obviously, you may think, the variable area now contains values for a, b and c, and these are occupying the extra 12 bytes. *Wrong!*

Look at the third line of your program again. The expression on the right of the equals sign (PEEK the system variable E-LINE) is evaluated first, and then the variable c is set equal to this value. So, at the time you actually find the end of the variable area, it only contains a and b, c has not yet been assigned.

RUN the program again, and when it has finished, enter GO TO 0 (to re-run without clearing the variables). Now you will see the true address of E-LINE, 6 bytes higher than before, i.e., the variable area occupies a total of 19 bytes; 6 each for the three variables, and one for the CHR$ 118.

Well, now that you know *where* the Timex Sinclair will store your program and variables, let's put some real programs there and find out exactly *what* it does store.

READER 1

We know where a program is stored in the Timex Sinclair's memory: in the area between PROG and VARS; and we can find the actual addresses of PROG and VARS by PEEKing the appropriate system variables. Therefore, by PEEKing all the addresses between PROG and VARS, we should be able to find our program.

Reader 1 is a general all-purpose PEEKer program which, given a start and finish address (in lines 10 and 15), will PEEK all the addresses in between. However, the program area is a logical place to start PEEKing, because, here at least, we know what we would expect to find. You would, after all, expect the program to be stored in exactly the same form as it was entered. (Wouldn't you?)

Run the program and see. (All the programs in this section, except "Renumber", will work on themselves, or on any other program which is in memory at the same time. So when you get bored with "reading" through "Reader 1", you can MERGE another program, provided that there are no clashes of line number, and read through that as well).

The output of the program is in three columns: column 1 lists every address between PROG and VARS, column 2 gives the contents of these addresses when PEEKed, and column 3 gives the CHARACTER represented by the peeked values.

For any other area of memory, column 3 would not be very

informative, but for the program area, it is this column which should reveal the program exactly as it was entered.

Of course, it doesn't. But although there are a few mysterious characters, and one or two unprintables (these are not rude words, but color control character which would probably cause an error report if they were attempted to be printed), there is enough similarity between column 3 and your original program for it to be obviously recognizable. Some of it has been stored exactly as you entered it, but some has been stored in a rather odd manner.

See if you can explain what has happened, and account for the odd characters, before entering "Reader 2".

```
READER 1

10 LET p=PEEK 23635+256*PEEK 23636
15 LET v=PEEK 23627+256*PEEK 23628
20 LET c=PEEK p
25 PRINT p;TAB 8;c;: IF c<16 OR c>23 THEN PRINT
       TAB 16;CHR$ c: GO TO 35
30 PRINT TAB 16;"(unprintable)"
35 LET p=p+1: IF p=v THEN STOP
40 GO TO 20
9000 SAVE "READER 1" LINE 0
```

READER 2

This is an amended version of the previous program, in which column 3 will give you your program listing exactly. (There may still be a few unprintables if you use color controls to make your programs list in pretty colors; "Reader 3", if you want to write that one yourself, could account for these as well.)

As you will have seen from "Reader 1", the main differences between a program in memory, and a program as entered or LISTed, lies in the way that numbers are stored. The Timex Sinclair distinguishes between line numbers and all other numbers, and stores them very differently.

LINE NUMBERS (i.e. the numbers *preceding* each program line. Line numbers which follow a GO TO or a GO SUB are stored in the same way as other numbers.)

Line numbers are stored as two-byte hexadecimal numbers. Numbers which require less than two bytes, i.e. numbers less than 256 decimal, are stored with a leading zero.

So, the first modification for "Reader 2" is that whenever a line number is encountered, two bytes of memory are converted to a single decimal number (see lines 20 and 25).

The two bytes which follow a line number are *not* part of your program listing. They are inserted by the computer to indicate the *length* (in number of bytes) of the program line, and hence act as a *pointer* to the next address which is to be treated as a line number.

Again these two bytes represent a hexadecimal number, but, just to confuse you, in case you were finding all this too easy, they are stored in *reverse* order. The high order byte (i.e., the one whose value must be multiplied by 256 when converting to decimal) is stored *after* the low order byte. This may sound illogical, but you will find as you explore deeper into the Timex Sinclair's memory, it is the normal way for the computer to store 2-byte numbers, and in fact it is LINE NUMBERS which are stored oddly.

OTHER NUMBERS

All other numbers are stored in the program area twice. First they are stored merely as characters, (e.g. 1.2 is stored as CHR$ 49;CHR$ 46;CHR$ 50). Then, a CHR$ 14 is stored to indicate that these characters do in fact form a number, and then the value of the number is stored in the next five bytes, using either integer or floating point format. We shall see the difference between these two formats in the program "Vars", but for the present, suffice it to say that whenever the character CHR$ 14 appears in the program area, we, and the computer, know that the next five bytes represent the value of a number (see line 50).

```
READER 2

10 LET p=PEEK 23635+256*PEEK 23636
15 LET v=PEEK 23627+256*PEEK 23628
20 LET n=256*PEEK p+PEEK (p+1)
25 GO SUB 100: PRINT n;TAB 21;"< LINE ": LET p=p+1:
        GO SUB 100: PRINT TAB 21;"< NUMBER": LET p=p+1
30 LET le= PEEK p+256* PEEK (p+1)
35 GO SUB 100: PRINT le;TAB 21;"< LINE ": LET p=p+1:
        GO SUB 100: PRINT TAB 21;"< LENGTH": LET p=p+1
40 LET le=p+le
45 LET c=PEEK p
50 GO SUB 100: IF c=14 THEN RESTORE : PRINT TAB 21;
        "NUMBER:":  FOR j=1 TO 5: LET p=p+1: GO SUB 100:
        READ n$: PRINT TAB 21;n$: NEXT j: GO TO 65
55 IF c<16 OR c>23 THEN PRINT ,TAB 16;CHR$ c: GO TO 65
60 PRINT TAB 16;"(unprintable)"
65 LET p=p+1: IF p=v THEN STOP
70 IF p=le THEN GO TO 20
75 GO TO 45
100 PRINT p;TAB 8;PEEK p;TAB 16;: RETURN
200 DATA "FIVE","BYTE","EQUIV.","OF","NUMBER"
9000 SAVE "READER 2" LINE 0
```

TRACE

It is very interesting to be able to read through the Timex Sinclair's program area, but is it actually any use? Do the last two programs offer any additional facilities not provided by the Basic command, LIST?

Not as they stand, perhaps, but now that we know the exact memory location of every part of the program, it is possible to search through the program area, and pinpoint the location of any particular keyword, number, variable, or whatever.

As it is listed here, "Trace" will locate specific variables used in a program, identifying the line number and statement in which they occur. You can easily modify the program to trace keywords or numbers, but I have chosen variables because you will probably find this most useful. (One of the commonest program bugs is caused by using the same variable name for two or more supposedly different variables.) Also, tracing variables is slightly more complex than tracing anything else, as variables with similar names (e.g., b, b$, bc and ab) must be distinguished between (see lines 75 and 80).

Some of the other pitfalls to avoid when "tracing" a particular item are:

a. Bytes which form part of a line number, line length, or numeric value should be ignored. You saw in "Reader 1" that the character represented by these bytes is irrelevant when taken out of context, and could easily be the same as the character for which we are searching (see lines 35 and 55).

b. Anything which occurs within quotes should also be ignored. Obviously you will want to use words like "a" in PRINT or INPUT statements, without these being identified as variable names (You have also probably found that, with a little keyboard manipulation, keywords like THEN or RUN can be used within text statements. These would be stored as single-byte keywords by the computer, but again you would not want them to be identified as keywords by a trace program.) This problem is avoided by the use of a quote flag, q in lines 35, 45, and 50. When the quotes are opened, q=1, and q=0 when they are closed.

Line 30 of the program is not necessary; it merely indicates the current line being "read" (just to reassure you that the program has not crashed between "finds").

As well as searching for the variable you have specified, the program also searches for the colon, outside quotation marks again, so that the statement number (c) within a line may be identified.

TRACE

```
5 INPUT "Variable to trace ";v$: LET l=LEN v$
10 LET p=PEEK 23635+256*PEEK 23636
15 LET v=PEEK 23627+256*PEEK 23628
20 LET n=256*PEEK p+PEEK (p+1)
25 LET le=PEEK (p+2)+256*PEEK (p+3)
30 PRINT n
35 LET a=0: LET c=1: FOR j=4 TO le+4
40 LET p1=PEEK (p+j)
45 IF p1=34 THEN LET a=NOT a
50 IF a THEN GO TO 90
55 IF p1=14 THEN LET j=j+5: GO TO 90
60 IF p1=58 THEN LET c=c+1
65 IF p1<>CODE v$(1) THEN GO TO 90
70 FOR k=1 TO l
75 LET p1=PEEK (p+j+k-1): IF p1<>CODE v$(k) THEN GO TO 90
80 NEXT k: LET k=PEEK (p+j+k-1): IF k=36 OR (k>47 AND
        k<58) OR (k>64 AND k<91) OR (k>96 AND k<123)
        THEN GO TO 90
85 PRINT FLASH 1; INK 2; PAPER 7;n;: PRINT INK 9;
        TAB 5;":";c;TAB 10;v$
90 NEXT j
95 LET p=4+p+le: IF p=v THEN STOP
100 GO TO 20
9000 SAVE "TRACE" LINE 0
```

RENUMBER

So far in this section we have "read" through the program area of the Timex Sinclair's RAM, and have pinpointed the exact memory locations corresponding to particular elements of a Basic program.

The next step is to actually change the contents of some of those memory locations; instead of merely PEEKing the program area, we will now POKE new values into it. It is now a Basic program which changes itself as it runs. Perhaps the most obvious example of this is a line renumbering routine.

We have already seen how line numbers can be identified in the program area; they *always* consist of two bytes, and they are always followed by two further bytes which point to the next line number (or, in the case of the last line of a program, to VARS). So, to renumber a program, all that is necessary is for appropriate new values to be POKEd into the locations containing the original line numbers (not forgetting to first convert the new line numbers from decimal to two-byte hexadecimal—see line 8).

NOTE: This method of line renumbering does not alter GO TO and GO SUB destinations. You must change these manually to match the new line numbers. For this reason, the program will not work on itself; hence the conditions in lines 1 and 3: the first line to be renumbered, and its new number, must be beyond the last line of the renumbering routine. There is no restriction on the last line to be renumbered, as the program will stop *either* when it reaches a line number beyond the one specified, *or* when it reaches VARS. Therefore, if you want to renumber an entire program, enter 9999 in response to the last line prompt.

```
RENUMBER

1 INPUT "First line to renumber ";f: IF f<10 THEN GO TO 1
2 INPUT "Last line to renumber ";e
3 INPUT ("New number for ";f;" ");r: IF r<10 THEN GO TO 3
4 INPUT "Step ";s: IF s<1 THEN GO TO 4
5 LET p=PEEK 23635+256*PEEK 23636: LET v=PEEK 23637+
        256*PEEK 23628
6 LET n=256*PEEK p+PEEK (p+1): LET l=PEEK (p+2)+256*
        PEEK (p+3): IF n<f THEN GO TO 9
7 IF n>e or p=v THEN LIST: STOP
8 LET p1=INT (r/256): POKE p,p1: POKE p+1,r-(p1*256):
        LET r=r+s
9 LET p=4+p+l: GO TO 6
9000 SAVE "RENUMBER" LINE 0
```

CASE SWAP

Of course, it is not just line numbers which can be altered by POKEing into the program area. Any particular item can be located, and if it can be located, then it can also be changed.

I will leave you to think of some of the more bizarre implications of this, but here is a useful routine which allows programs to be LISTed in either upper or lower case.

You will have noticed that all the programs in this book have been listed in lower case, so that you can distinguish between variable names and keywords (which are *always* listed in upper case). However, if you have worked with other computers, particularly those which do not have lower case at all, or find that lower case letters like "m" or "l" are difficult to read, you may prefer to use "Case Swap" to convert listings to upper case once they have been entered. (Or, alternatively, to enter the programs with CAPS SHIFT on, and then use "Case Swap" to make them correspond exactly to those in the book.)

"Case Swap" converts *all* lower case letters to upper case (or vice versa), including variable names *and* text. You may, if you prefer, use a quote flag system (as in "Trace") to leave text unaltered.

The two key lines in "Case Swap" are:

Line 85: POKEs an upper case letter in place of a lower case one.

Line 90: POKEs a lower case letter in place of an upper case one.

CASE SWAP (Listed in lower case)

```
5 CLS: PRINT''"to list in lower case, press ""l"""
10 PRINT ''"to list in upper case, press ""u"""
15 LET i$=INKEY$
20 IF i$=CHR$ 108 OR i$=CHR$ 76 THEN LET l=1: GO TO 35
25 IF i$=CHR$ 117 OR i$=CHR$ 85 THEN LET l=0: GO TO 35
30 GO TO 15
35 CLS: PRINT FLASH 1;"reading through program"
40 DEF FN p(a)=PEEK a+256*PEEK (a+1)
45 LET prog=FN p(23635)
50 LET a=prog-5
55 LET a=a+5
60 LET p=PEEK a
65 IF a>=FN p(23627) THEN CLS: LIST : STOP
70 IF p=13 THEN GO TO 55
75 IF p=14 THEN LET a=a+1: GO TO 55
80 IF l THEN GO TO 90
85 IF p>=97 AND p<=122 THEN POKE a,p-32: GO TO 95
90 IF p>=65 AND p<=90 THEN POKE a,p+32
95 LET a=a+1: GO TO 60
9000 SAVE "case swap" LINE 0
```

CASE SWAP (Listed in upper case)

```
5 CLS: PRINT''"TO LIST IN LOWER CASE, PRESS ""L"""
10 PRINT ''"TO LIST IN UPPER CASE, PRESS ""U"""
15 LET I$=INKEY$
20 IF I$=CHR$ 108 OR I$=CHR$ 76 THEN LET L=1: GO TO 35
25 IF I$=CHR$ 117 OR I$=CHR$ 85 THEN LET L=0: GO TO 35
30 GO TO 15
35 CLS: PRINT FLASH 1;"READING THROUGH PROGRAM"
40 DEF FN P(A)=PEEK A+256*PEEK (A+1)
45 LET PROG=FN P(23635)
50 LET A=PROG-5
55 LET A=A+5
60 LET P=PEEK A
65 IF A>=FN P(23627) THEN CLS: LIST : STOP
70 IF P=13 THEN GO TO 55
75 IF P=14 THEN LET A=A+1: GO TO 55
80 IF L THEN GO TO 90
85 IF P>=97 AND P<=122 THEN POKE A,P-32: GO TO 95
90 IF P>=65 AND P<=90 THEN POKE A,P+32
95 LET A=A+1: GO TO 60
9000 SAVE "CASE SWAP" LINE 0
```

VARS

By now you have probably had just about enough of the program area, so let's move on to the area between VARS and E-LINE, known as the variable area or variable store.

You will notice immediately that this program is considerably longer than any of the previous programs in this section. The reason for this is that variables are stored in a very concise format, and so decoding the bytes in the variable store is considerably more complex than decoding those in the program area.

The byte (or bytes) containing the variable name is not simply stored as the CODE for that name. It also contains information as to the TYPE OF VARIABLE, and hence the number and format of the bytes which follow. The different types of variable which the Timex Sinclair can handle are listed below (and there are more of them than you might think).

Numbers	**Example**
Integer variables with a single letter name	a
Integer variables with a two character name	ab
Integer variables with a multi-character name	abcd
Floating point variables with a single letter name	a
Floating point variables with a two character name	ab
Floating point variables with a multi-character name	abcd
Loop control variables	a
Numeric array	a()
Strings	**Example**
Undimensioned string	a$
String array	a$()

Notice that we, the users, cannot distinguish, simply by looking at the variable name, between integers, floating point numbers, and loop control variables. We can't, but the Timex Sinclair can.

One thing that all variables have in common is that they must begin with a letter, and that lower case and upper case are not differentiated between. That makes only 26 possibilities (for the first letter of a name, at least), and any number up to 26 can be stored in only five bits. (Convert 26 to binary form to prove this). Therefore, three bits of the name-byte are available to indicate the type of variable.

You may not be used to thinking of bytes as 8-bit binary numbers, but you must get into this habit if you are to understand the variable store. Line 30 strips the five lowest bytes (the name itself) off the name-byte, leaving a number in the range (decimal) 2 and 7. The REM statements in lines 35 to 60 indicate which type of variable has thus been identified, and these lines also contain a branch to the appropriate evaluation routine.

Routine 100: Numbers—Single character name

This routine merely calls subroutine 800, which first determines whether the number is an integer or floating point. The five bytes following the name represent the value of the variable, and are stored in exactly the same format as in the program area. If the first byte is zero, then the number is an integer, and the evaluation is relatively simple (line 825). Lines 850 to 870 perform the more complex calculation to evaluate floating point numbers.

Routine 200: Number—More than one character name

Line 200 applies the correction needed to display the first letter of the name. (I have used the convention of displaying all numeric variable names in lower case, and all strings in upper case. You should realize by now why this convention is purely arbitrary, and why the Timex Sinclair does not distinguish between the two).

Line 230 identifies the last letter of the name (highest bit=1). Line 240 prints any intermediate letters. Line 260 prints the last letter. The routine then branches to line 100 for evaluation as before.

Routine 300: Number arrays

Again, line 300 applies the correction to display the array name. Subroutine 900 (also used for string arrays) reads the number of dimensions (d), the size of each dimension (el), and calculates the total number of elements (t).

Subroutine 800 is then called t times, to evaluate each element in turn.

Routine 400: Loop Control

The variable store holds far more information about loop control variables than merely their current value. Line 410 evaluates the variable as normal. Lines 425 to 430 reads the limit value. Lines 435 to 440 read the STEP. Lines 450 to 460 read the line and statement number of the looping line.

Routine 500: Strings

Line 510 reads the LENgth of the string, and lines 520 to 540 print its characters.

Routine 600: String array

This routine uses subroutine 900 to print the size of the array, and then merely prints the character of each element.

This program is very long, but by using it you will gain considerable insight into the way that data is stored by the computer, and the way in which the computer interprets that data.

The program will work on itself, though the results may not always be what you would expect (remember that the contents of the variable store are being up-dated as the program is running). Try setting up some dummy variables in line 1, and investigate how these are stored. See what happens if you make line 1:

```
1 LET x=1.1234567890123 45
```

```
VARS

5 DIM b(5)
10 LET p=PEEK 23627+256*PEEK 23628
20 PRINT p;TAB 6;: LET p1=PEEK p
25 IF p1=128 THEN PRINT TAB 7;"END OF VARIABLE AREA": STOP
30 LET p2=INT (p1/32)
35 IF p2=3 THEN GO TO 100: REM number (single-letter name)
40 IF p2=5 THEN GO TO 200: REM number (multi-character name)
45 IF p2=4 THEN GO TO 300: REM number array
50 IF p2=7 THEN GO TO 400: REM loop control
55 IF p2=2 THEN GO TO 500: REM string
60 IF p2=6 THEN GO TO 600: REM string array
70 STOP: REM error if this line is reached
100 REM number:-
105 PRINT CHR$ p1;
```

[continued]

```
110 GO SUB 800
115 PRINT TAB 16;n
120 LET p=p+1: GO TO 20
200 PRINT CHR$ (p1-64);: REM first letter
210 LET p=p+1
220 LET p1=PEEK p
230 IF p1>=128 THEN GO TO 260
240 PRINT CHR$ p1;: REM middle letters (if any)
250 GO TO 210
260 PRINT CHR$ (p1-128);: REM last letter
270 GO TO 110
300 PRINT CHR$ (p1-32);"(";
305 GO SUB 900
310 FOR k=1 TO t
315 GO SUB 800
320 PRINT TAB 3;"element #";k;TAB 16;n
325 NEXT k
330 LET p=p+1: GO TO 20
400 PRINT CHR$ (p1-128);
410 GO SUB 800
420 PRINT TAB 9;"(LOOP)";TAB 16;n;TAB 22;"Current"
425 GO SUB 800
430 PRINT TAB 16;n;TAB 22;"Limit (TO)"
435 GO SUB 800
440 PRINT TAB 16;n;TAB 22;"STEP"
450 LET l=PEEK (p+1)+256*PEEK (p+2): LET s=PEEK (p+3):
       LET p=p+4
455 PRINT TAB 16;l;TAB 22;"Line No."
460 PRINT TAB 16;s;TAB 22;"Statement"
465 GO TO 20
500 PRINT CHR$ p1;"$";TAB 16;
510 LET l=PEEK (p+1)+256*PEEK (p+2): LET p=p+2
520 FOR j=1 TO l
530 PRINT CHR$ PEEK (p+j);
540 NEXT j: PRINT
550 LET p=p+j: GO TO 20
600 PRINT CHR$ (p1-128);"$(";
605 GO SUB 900
610 FOR k=1 TO t
620 LET p=p+1
630 PRINT TAB 3;"element #";k;TAB 16;CHR$ PEEK p
640 NEXT k
650 LET p=p+1: GO TO 20
800 REM integer
805 FOR j=1 TO 5
810 LET p=p+1: LET b(j)=PEEK p
815 NEXT j
820 IF b(1) THEN GO TO 845
825 LET n=b(3)+256*b(4): IF b(2)=255 THEN LET n=n-65536
830 RETURN
845 REM floating point
850 LET m=1: IF b(2)<128 THEN LET m=0: LET b(2)=b(2)+128
855 LET n=0: FOR j=2 TO 5: LET n=n+b(j)/256↑(j-1): NEXT j
860 LET b(1)=b(1)-128
865 LET n=n*2↑b(1)
870 IF m THEN LET n=-n
875 RETURN
```

```
900 REM arrays
905 LET p1=PEEK (p+1)+256*PEEK (p+2): LET p=p+3
910 LET d=PEEK p: LET p=p+1
915 LET t=1: FOR j=1 TO d
920 LET el=PEEK p+256*PEEK (p+1): LET t=t*el: PRINT el;
925 IF d<>1 AND j<>d THEN PRINT",";
930 LET p=p+2: NEXT j: PRINT ")"
940 LET p=p-1
945 RETURN
9000 SAVE "VARS" LINE 0
```

5

The Very Pulse of the Machine

- RENUMBER
- COLOR RESET
- PAGES—STORE AND RECALL (48K)
- SCROLL—LEFT/RIGHT

RENUMBER

All the programs in the previous section run very slowly. Try renumbering a long program with the Basic "Renumber" routine and it will take forever (or so it will seem). Sounds like a job for . . . MACHINE CODE.

Here is the same routine, simplified slightly. This version renumbers the *entire* program, in five steps, the first new line becoming line number 5. You can change the step by altering the appropriate byte of code i.e., the 17th item in the DATA statement.

The Basic Loader program will locate the machine code, starting at address 32000, so to call the renumber routine, use:

```
RANDOMIZE USR 32000
```

When you SAVE the loader, using GO TO 9000, you will be asked to save both the Loader program (for your library—you will not actually need the Loader again) and the machine code routine itself.

To LOAD the machine code at some later date, use:

```
CLEAR 31999: LOAD "RENUMBER"CODE 32000,31
```

(48k users may of course, locate this routine at a very much higher address. Remember that you can SAVE bytes from one address, and LOAD them into another, so there is no need to alter the Basic Loader from the version printed.)

RENUMBER

Mnemonic	DECIMAL code	Effect
LD HL,(23635)	42,83,92	HL=PROG
LD DE,0	17,0,0	DE=0
LD BC,(23627)	237,75,75,92	BC=VARS
AND A	167	CLEAR CARRY
SBC HL,BC	237,66	IS HL=VARS?
RET Z	200	IF YES, RETURN
ADD HL,BC	9	RESTORE VALUE OF HL
LD B,5	6,5	B=5 (STEP)
INC DE	19	INCREASE DE BY STEP
DJNZ,-3	16,253	DE=NEW LINE NUMBER
LD (HL),D	114	INSERT
INC HL	35	NEW
LD (HL),E	115	LINE NUMBER
INC HL	35	BC
LD C,(HL)	78	=
INC HL	35	LINE
LD B,(HL)	70	LENGTH
ADD HL,BC	9	HL=NEXT
INC HL	35	LINE NUMBER
JR,-25	24,231	REPEAT

BASIC LOADER

```
1 RESTORE: CLEAR 31999: LET j=32000
2 READ a: IF a=9999 THEN STOP
3 POKE j,a: LET j=j+1: GO TO 2
500 DATA 42,83,92,17,0,0,237,75,75,92,167,237,66,200,9,
        6,5,19,16,253,114,35,115,35,78,35,70,9,35,24,231
9000 SAVE "RENUMBER" LINE 0
9005 SAVE "RENUMBER"CODE 32000,31
9999 DATA 9999
```

COLOR RESET

How many times have you LISTed a program, only to find that it is printed in cyan INK on magenta PAPER, or worse still, black INK on black PAPER?

Here is a very simple USR routine which will reset the screen colors to good old white BORDER, white PAPER, black INK, regardless of the colors that may have been left by the program.

As well as being useful during debugging, it might be nice to include this USR call at the end of your programs, so that the user can read your listings without suffering severe eye strain.

All the routine does is load the two System Variables BORDER and ATTR P with the value 56 (which equals white BORDER, or, as you will remember from "ATTR Table", black INK on white PAPER).

IMPORTANT NOTE

Here is another way to make your listings readable, without resorting to machine code:

Enter line number 1
Press both shifts and key "7"
Press both shifts, hold down CAPS SHIFT and press key "0"
Press ENTER

Line 1 will appear as a blank line in your listing, but all subsequent lines will be listed in black INK on white PAPER.

COLOR RESET

Mnemonic	DECIMAL code	Effect
LD BC,23624	1,72,92	BC=BORDER
LD A,56	62,56	56=WHITE BORDER
LD (BC),A	2	SET BORDER
LD C,141	14,141	BC=23693=ATTR P
LD (BC),A	2	SET PAPER, INK
RET	201	RETURN

BASIC LOADER

```
10 CLEAR 31999
20 RESTORE: FOR j=32000 TO 32009
30 READ a: POKE j,a: NEXT j: STOP
100 DATA 1,72,92,62,56,2,14,141,2,201
9000 SAVE "RESET" LINE 0
9005 SAVE "RESET"CODE 32000,10
```

PAGES—STORE AND RECALL (48K)

Some computers have a paging facility, whereby several different screen displays may be stored and recalled instantly. So does the Timex Sinclair, if you use this short machine code routine.

"Store" copies a screen display into a reserved area of memory (above RAMTOP), and "Recall" simply copies it back again. You will notice that the two routines are almost identical, and both illustrate the power and speed of the LDIR instruction which is used to copy nearly 7000 bytes in a fraction of a second.

The Basic program is more than just a loader; it also includes two subroutines which actually change the machine code program to point to the correct part of reserved memory for the required page.

Subroutine 1000 will STORE screen pages at addresses 33000, 40000, 47000 and 54000 (pages 1 to 4 respectively). Subroutine 2000 will RECALL any one of these four pages.

You can incorporate "Pages" into other programs, to instantly store and recall screen displays as required, or you can create a catalogue of your favorite displays. Remember that once a display has been loaded into reserved memory, you can delete the actual program which created it, and still recall the display by using GO SUB 2000.

Line 9005 saves not only the machine code routines, but also the *entire* page storage area.

PAGES

STORE		RECALL	
Mnemonic	DECIMAL code	Mnemonic	DECIMAL code
LD DE,33000	17,232,128	LD DE,16384	17,0,64
LD HL,16384	33,0,64	LD HL,33000	33,232,128
LD BC,6912	1,0,27	same	same
LDIR	237,176	same	same
RET	201	same	same

LOADER/"CALL" SUBROUTINES

```
10 CLEAR 31999: LET s=32000: LET r=32050
20 RESTORE: FOR j=0 TO 11: READ a: POKE s+j,a: NEXT j
30 FOR j=0 TO 11: READ a: POKE r+j,a: NEXT j: STOP
100 DATA 17,232,128,33,0,64,1,0,27,237,176,201
200 DATA 17,0,64,33,232,128,1,0,27,237,176,201
1000 INPUT "Store as page no. (1-4) ";p
1010 LET p=INT p: IF p<1 OR p>4 THEN GO TO 1000
1020 LET a=p*7000+26000: LET a2=INT (a/256): LET a1=a-a2*256
1030 POKE 32001,a1: POKE 32002,a2
1040 LET n=USR s
1050 RETURN
2000 INPUT "Recall page no. (1-4) ";p
2010 LET p=INT p: IF p<1 OR p>4 THEN GO TO 2000
2020 LET a=p*7000+26000: LET a2=INT (a/256): LET a1=a-a2*256
2030 POKE 32054,a1: POKE 32055,a2
2040 LET n=USR r
2050 RETURN
9000 SAVE "PAGES" LINE 0
9005 SAVE "PAGES"CODE 32000,30000
```

SCROLL—LEFT/RIGHT

These two routines use the instructions RL (HL) and RR (HL) to rotate the screen displays, thereby creating a very attractive left or right scroll effect.

The Basic program includes the loader (lines 10 to 60), and also a demonstration of the routine in action (lines 5 and 100 to 130).

Notice that the limit of the FOR TO loop (lines 105 and 120) is *eight times* the number of characters to be scrolled off screen.

The RL and RR instructions (Rotate Left and Rotate Right) have some close relations in machine code, and some interesting effects (though *not* scrolls) can be achieved by substituting these. (Alter the *eighth* data item in lines 50 and 60.)

Try:

Rotate and Carry (RLC/RRC)
Change "22" to "6" in line 50. Change "30" to "14" in line 60.

This creates a screen ripple as each character rotates about its own axis.

Shift (SLA/SRA)
Change "22" to "38" in line 50 or "30" to "46" in line 60.

This creates a Venetian blind effect as each character rotates itself off screen.

SCROLL

LEFT		RIGHT	
Mnemonic	DECIMAL code	Mnemonic	DECIMAL CODE
LD HL,22527	33,255,87	LD HL,16384	33,0,64
LD C,32	14,32	same	same
AND A	167	same	same
RL (HL)	203,22	RR (HL)	203,30
DEC HL	43	INC HL	35
DEC C	13	same	same
JRNZ,-5	32,250	same	same
LD A,63	62,63	LD A,88	62,88
CP H	188	same	same
JRNZ,-13	32,242	same	same
RET	201	same	same
NOP	0		
NOP	0		

LOADER/DEMO

```
5 BORDER 6: PAPER 6: INK 2: CLS
10 CLEAR 31999
20 LET j=32000
30 READ a: IF a=9999 THEN GO TO 100
40 POKE j,a: LET j=j+1: GO TO 30
50 DATA 33,255,87,14,32,167,203,22,43,13,32,250,62,
        63,188,32,242,201,0,0
60 DATA 33,0,64,14,32,167,203,30,35,13,32,250,62,
        88,188,32,242,201
100 FOR j=1 TO 22: PRINT "qwertyuiopasdfghjklzxcvbnm
        123456": NEXT j
105 FOR j=1 TO 8*16
110 RANDOMIZE USR 32020
115 NEXT j
120 FOR j=1 TO 8*16
125 RANDOMIZE USR 32000
130 NEXT j: STOP
9000 SAVE "SCROLL" LINE 0
9005 SAVE "SCROLL"CODE 32000,38
9999 DATA 9999
```

6

Interlude

- OVERS 1 (EXPERIMENTS)
- OVERS 2 (GAME)
- PATTERNS 1 (KALEIDOSCOPE)
- PATTERNS 2 (MOIRE)
- INVERT

OVERS 1 (EXPERIMENTS)

There are many examples of User Defined Graphics in this book, but if you just want to create an odd shaped character for some reason there is a very easy way to do so without all that USR CHR$ 144 business. Just use the EXCLUSIVE OR aspect of the expression OVER 1 to print one character on top of another, obliterating all points where the two characters meet.

This program allows you to enter any two characters. Line 50 will show you the two characters plus the strange EXCLUSIVE-OR character created by OVER 1. Useful, eh? In fact, you will be surprised how easy it is to create some interesting "invader" type characters by using this method.

```
OVERS 1

10 PRINT "EXPERIMENTS WITH "" OVER """''
20 INPUT "Enter any 2 characters (or space to stop) ";a$
30 IF a$=CHR$ 32 THEN STOP
40 IF LEN a$<>2 THEN GO TO 20
50 PRINT a$(1);CHR$ 8; OVER 1;a$(2);"  =  ";a$(1);
       "  OVER  ";a$(2)
60 GO TO 20
9000 SAVE "OVERS 1" LINE 0
```

OVERS 2 (GAME)

The second program is a game (of sorts), designed once again, to help you become familiar with the implications of the OVER 1 statement.

Line 30 puts an incomplete row of $ signs across the center of the screen.

You have control of the flashing $ sign and, using the direction arrow keys (5 and 8), can move this sign left and right over the others.

The ultimate object of the game is to create either a complete row of $ signs, or a completely blank line.

As an intermediate objective, however, you might try to explain exactly what is happening, why some characters are erased and others printed, and just what control you have to affect these events.

```
OVERS 2

10 OVER 1: BORDER 1: PAPER 5: INK 9: CLS
20 LET b=0
30 FOR j=1 TO 31: PRINT AT 11,j;"$": LET j=j+RND*3: NEXT j
40 LET b=b+(INKEY$="8" AND b<>31)-(INKEY$="5" AND b<>0)
50 PRINT AT 11,b;"$"
60 GO TO 40
9000 SAVE "OVERS 2" LINE 0
```

PATTERNS 1 (KALEIDOSCOPE)

I am sure you can think of much more useful things to do with your Timex Sinclair than create pretty patterns on the screen. You can't? All right then, here are two programs which do just that. The first program creates kaleidoscope patterns.

Line 60 plots the four symmetrical points. OVER 1 (line 10) means that points are unplotted as well as plotted, so the screen never actually fills up.

```
PATTERNS 1

10 OVER 1: RANDOMIZE
20 BORDER 0: PAPER 0: CLS
30 LET x=RND*128
40 LET y=RND*88
50 INK RND*7: BRIGHT INT (RND*2)
60 PLOT x,y: PLOT 255-x,y: PLOT x,175-y: PLOT 255-x,175-y
70 IF INKEY$="" THEN GO TO 30
80 STOP
9000 SAVE "PATTERNS 1" LINE 0
```

PATTERNS 2 (MOIRE)

"Patterns 2" create moire or interference patterns caused by the drawing of near-parallel lines using the OVER 1 condition.

NOTE: It is difficult to create a moire program which will run continuously, as usually the OVER 1 statement will eventually cause the pattern to be deleted from the screen. By cycling through four patterns however, the screen is never totally cleared by this program.

The INK color is changed at the end of each cycle of four patterns in line 20. Statement 2 of line 20 prevents the same INK color being repeated.

```
PATTERNS 2

5 OVER 1: BORDER 0: PAPER 0: INK 2: CLS
10 GO SUB 100
15 LET a=2
20 LET i=INT (RND*7)+1: IF i=a THEN GO TO 20
25 INK i: LET a=i: GO SUB 200: GO SUB 100: GO SUB 100:
      GO SUB 200: GO TO 20
100 FOR x=0 TO 255
105 PLOT x,0: DRAW 255-x,175: PLOT 255-x,175: DRAW x-255,-175
110 NEXT x
115 RETURN
200 FOR x=0 TO 255
205 PLOT x,175: DRAW 255-x,-175: PLOT 255-x,0: DRAW x-255,175
210 NEXT x
215 RETURN
9000 SAVE "PATTERNS 2" LINE 0
```

INVERT

This program does not really belong in the silly section at all, as it actually illustrates a very useful feature of the Timex Sinclair. It is just that the example I have chosen to demonstrate this feature is incredibly silly.

You might think that the Timex Sinclair will only allow 21 User Defined Graphics, but in fact the entire character set can be User Defined, so if you want to print in Greek, Russian, or even Chinese, you can do so.

The technique is to alter the contents of the System Variable CHARS from its normal value (an address in ROM) to some other address (preferably above RAMTOP) where your own character definitions are located (see line 70).

This new character set can be created in exactly the same way as all other User Defined Characters (i.e., eight bytes defining each character), but for this program I have cheated by making an exact copy of the normal Timex Sinclair character set. Well, *almost* an exact copy. Line 40 ensures that all the characters are copied *upside down*.

The results are highly amusing, and might well cause some consternation should you (accidentally, of course), run this program on a friend's Timex Sinclair, or on a display model in a shop.

Interestingly, the fact that the computer now prints everything upside down (including its own report codes) does not affect its working in any way. You can even LOAD and run another program, which will work perfectly but will use the inverted characters.

The program takes several seconds to run, but once you have created the new character set, you can switch between the two sets instantly. Use GO TO 9995 to return to the normal characters, and GO TO 70 for the inverted set.

```
INVERT

5 CLEAR 29999
10 LET c=PEEK 23606+256*PEEK 23607+256
20 FOR j=0 TO 95
30 FOR p=0 TO 7
40 POKE 30000+7-p+8*j,PEEK (c+p+8*j)
50 NEXT p
60 NEXT j
70 POKE 23606,48: POKE 23607,116
80 STOP
9000 SAVE "INVERT" LINE 0
9995 REM recovery
9996 POKE 23606,0: POKE 23607,60
```

PROBLEM

Can you join these 16 dots with only 6 straight lines, without taking your pencil off the paper?

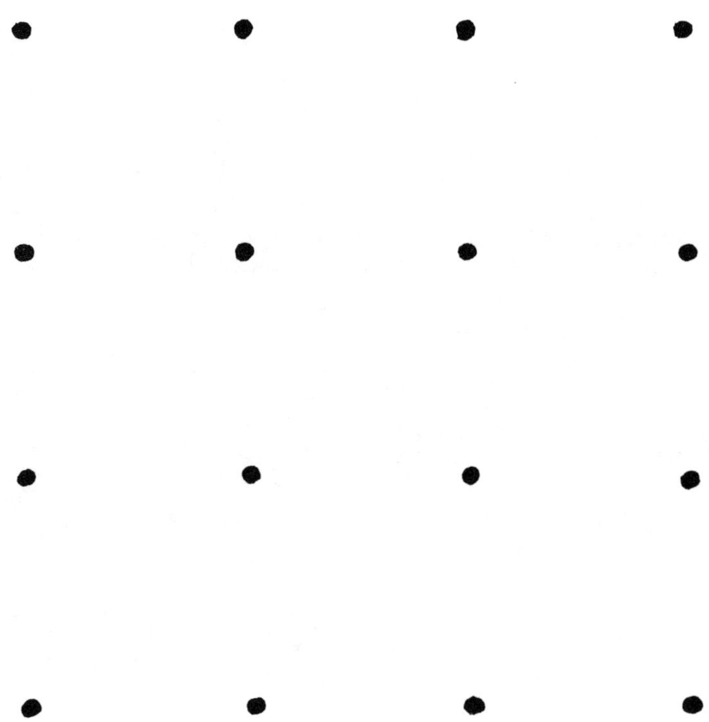

Solution

```
10 FOR x=70 TO 160 STEP 30
15 FOR y=50 TO 140 STEP 30
20 PLOT x,y
25 NEXT y: NEXT x
30 PRINT AT 20,3;"Press any key for solution": PAUSE 0
40 PLOT 160,140
50 RESTORE: FOR j=1 TO 6: READ a,b: DRAW a,b: PAUSE 20:
        NEXT j: STOP
100 DATA -60,0,0,-90,90,0,-120,120,0,-150,90,90
9000 SAVE "SOLUTION" LINE 0
```

7

A Matter of Routine

- INPUT 1 AND INPUT 2
- SORT
- LEAGUE TABLE
- CASH
- LOCATE A RECORD

INPUT 1 AND 2

The way in which Timex Sinclair handles the command INPUT is different from, and in some ways inferior to, that of many computers.

The input prompt appears at the bottom of the screen, and as soon as you press ENTER, both the prompt and your entry disappear. This is not always desirable, particularly in "questionnaire" type programs where the user might want to look back over the previous questions and answers.

"Input 1" and "Input 2" are two subroutines which each offer an alternative to the straightforward INPUT statement. "Input 1" duplicates the conventional form of INPUT found on most computers, where the input prompt and response are postioned at a specified place on the screen, and remain there when the input is completed.

"Input 2", which is also known as Hangman-style input, does not produce a prompt, but gives a row of dashes which are replaced by characters as you press the keys. The input is terminated either by pressing ENTER or by reaching the end of the row of dashes. This method of input is ideal for entering data into a string array, (where the length is predetermined).

IMPORTANT NOTE

The first line of each routine merely establishes local variables for demonstration. If you use the routines in other programs, lines 8000/8100 should be amended, so that:

x and y are row and column where input is to appear.

In "Input 1" t$ is the prompt.

In "Input 2" t$ is the string array for which data is required.

l is the length of the string array.

Both routines return the user's entry in t$.

Program Notes

Both routines use concatenation to compile the string t$. Each new value of INKEY$ is added to the end of t$ except when the key pressed was either ENTER (CHR$ 13), which terminates the entry, or DELETE (CHR$ 12), which causes the last character to be omitted (lines 8040 and 8130).

```
INPUT 1

8000 LET x=10: LET y=0: LET t$="Name"
8005 PRINT AT x;y;t$
8010 LET y=y+2+LEN t$
8015 LET t$=""
8020 IF y>31 OR y=-1 THEN LET y=31*(y=-1): LET x=x-1+2*(y=0)
8025 PRINT AT x,y; FLASH 1;"?"
8030 PAUSE 0: LET a$=INKEY$
8035 IF a$=CHR$ 13 AND t$<>"" THEN GO TO 8065
8040 IF a$=CHR$ 12 AND t$<>"" THEN PRINT AT x,y;CHR$ 32:
     LET y=y-1: LET t$=t$( TO LEN t$-1): GO TO 8020
8045 IF a$< CHR$ 32 THEN GO TO 8030
8050 LET t$=t$+a$
8055 PRINT AT x,y;a$: LET y=y+1
8060 GO TO 8020
8065 PRINT AT x,y;CHR$ 32: RETURN
9000 SAVE "INPUT 1" LINE 0
```

```
INPUT 2

8100 LET x=5: LET n=10: LET l=15: DIM t$(n,l)
8105 FOR j=1 TO n: FOR k=1 TO l
8110 PRINT AT x+j-1,k;CHR$ 45
8115 NEXT k: LET k=1
8120 PAUSE 0: LET a$=INKEY$
8125 IF a$=CHR$ 13 AND k<>1 THEN GO TO 8150
8130 IF a$=CHR$ 12 AND k<>1 THEN LET k=k-1: PRINT AT
     x+j-1,k;CHR$ 45: LET t$(j)=t$(j, TO k): GO TO 8120
8135 IF a$<CHR$ 32 THEN GO TO 8120
8140 LET t$(j,k)=a$: PRINT AT x+j-1,k;a$: LET k=k+1
8145 IF k<=l THEN GO TO 8120
8150 NEXT j
8155 RETURN
9000 SAVE "INPUT 2" LINE 0
```

SORT

This is a simple method for sorting an array of numbers into descending order (or, with minor amendments, ascending order).

The method is a variation of the well-known bubble sort, and works as follows:

There are two nested loops; the outer, j, loop determines the number of passes through the array.

The inner, k, loop, compares each number in the array with the following number and if the second number is higher than the first, it swaps them over. At the end of the first pass, therefore, the smallest number is left as the last element of the array.

On the next pass (NEXT j), the k loop sorts the second-lowest number into the second-last array element, and so on until the final pass, when just the first two elements are sorted.

Lines 8200 and 8218 are not part of the "Sort" routine but are for demonstration. Twenty random numbers are listed on the left hand side of the screen, sorted, and then listed in descending order on the right hand side.

```
SORT

8200 LET n=20: DIM a(n): FOR j=1 TO n: LET a(j)=INT
          (RND*1000): PRINT j;TAB 5;a(j): NEXT j
8205 FOR j=1 TO n-1: FOR k=1 TO n-j
8210 IF a(k)<a(k+1) THEN LET t=a(k): LET a(k)=a(k+1):
          LET a(k+1)=t
8215 NEXT k: NEXT j
8218 FOR j=1 TO n: PRINT AT j-1,16;j;TAB 22;a(j): NEXT j:
          REM (for demo only)
8220 RETURN
9000 SAVE "SORT" LINE 0
```

LEAGUE TABLE

"League Table" is not actually a subroutine; it is a complete program in its own right, and it utilizes a modified version of the previous "Sort" routine. Nevertheless, it can be included in many other programs where a regularly updated points table is required, e.g., football leagues, election results etc.

As listed here, DATA line 8000 contains the number 22, followed by the twenty-two teams in the first division of an English football league, (except that I haven't bothered to list them all). Whatever you use the program for, the DATA should always consist of a number, followed by that number of items.

Line 10 READs the DATA into array t$($), but the first character of each element of t$ is reserved for the *score* for each team.

The main part of the program contains yet another form of input routine—this time, any numeric keypress will be interpreted as an input, or the DELETE key will erase the name of the current team and the score of the previous team, so that this may be amended.

The "Sort" subroutine is similar to the last program, except that here the first character of each element of t$ is extracted, converted to a number (using CODE), and then the whole array is sorted with reference to the relative value of these numbers. (Obviously this method will only work provided that it is not possible for a team to score more than 255 points. This is true of the English football league, but if higher scores are possible in your particular application then a two-byte number system would have to be used.)

After the sorted data is displayed, the whole program is SAVEd (line 240), so that the next time it is LOADed, new scores may be added to the previous totals.

LEAGUE TABLE

```
10 RESTORE 8000: READ n: DIM t$(n,14): FOR j=1 TO n:
        LET t$(j,1)=CHR$ 0: READ t$(j,2 TO ): NEXT j
20 DIM b$(13)
100 CLS: PRINT "Enter points scored this week:"
105 FOR j=1 TO n
110 LET x=INT ((j+1)/2): LET y=16*(j=x*2)
115 PRINT AT x,y;t$(j,2 TO );CHR$ 32;CHR$ 8;
120 PAUSE 0: LET p$=INKEY$
125 IF p$=CHR$ 12 AND j>1 THEN PRINT AT x,y;b$: LET j=j-1:
        LET t$(j,1)=CHR$ (CODE t$(j,1)-p): GO TO 110
130 IF p$<"0" OR p$>"9" THEN GO TO 120
135 PRINT p$
140 LET p=VAL p$: LET t$(j,1)=CHR$ (CODE t$(j,1)+p)
150 NEXT j: PRINT AT 15,11;"SORTING"
155 GO SUB 8200
200 CLS: FOR j=1 TO n
205 IF j<>1 THEN IF t$(j,1)=t$(j-1,1) THEN GO TO 215
210 PRINT j;
215 PRINT TAB 3;t$(j,2 TO );CODE t$(j,1)
220 NEXT j
230 INPUT "Press ""ENTER"" to save data ";a$
240 SAVE "LEAGUE" LINE 100
8000 DATA 22,"Arsenal","Aston Villa"...etc (see text)
8200 REM sort subroutine (modified)
8205 FOR j=1 TO n-1: FOR k=1 TO n-j
8207 LET a=CODE t$(k,1): LET b=CODE t$(k+1,1)
8210 IF a<b THEN LET a$=t$(k): LET t$(k)=t$(k+1):
        LET t$(k+1)=a$
8215 NEXT k: NEXT j
8220 RETURN
9000 SAVE "LEAGUE" LINE 0
```

CASH

One of the most useful of all subroutines, this converts unformated numbers into a consistent cash format, so that they may be positioned neatly in columns.

When calling the subroutine, variable p should contain a number. On return from the routine, m$ will contain the formated number.

m$ will always contain a decimal point at its sixth character, so all numbers, even integers, will appear to be printed to two decimal places.

The routine also embodies an error-trapping device (variable x). Whenever p could not have been a valid cash figure (i.e., had more than 2 places of decimals), x is set to 1, so that the main program can reject the figure.

The routine does not include any demonstration data, as it is included in two programs in this book, "Invoicing" and "Sales Ledger." However, if you want to test it, add lines:

```
10 INPUT p: GO SUB 5000
20 IF x=0 THEN PRINT m$
30 GO TO 10
```

CASH

```
5000 LET x=0: DIM m$(8): LET m$=STR$ p
5010 IF m$(8)=CHR$ 32 THEN LET m$=CHR$ 32+m$( TO 7): GO TO 5010
5020 FOR j=1 TO 8
5030 IF m$(j)="." THEN GO TO 5050
5040 NEXT j
5050 IF j=9 THEN LET m$=m$(4 TO )+".00"
5060 IF j=7 THEN LET m$=m$(2 TO )+"0"
5070 IF m$(6)<>"." THEN LET x=1
5080 RETURN
9000 SAVE "CASH" LINE 0
```

LOCATE A RECORD

This is an essential subroutine for any database type of program.

Line 8500, which is the usual demonstration only line, allows you to set up a mini-database of ten records and fifteen fields per record. The actual size of the database is irrelevant as all you are asked to enter in line 8500 is the first field (keyfield) for each record.

The routine asks you to enter the name of the record you want to examine, and then searches through all the keyfields until it finds that name. Nothing very clever about that . . . but what makes the routine useful is that if you only enter part of a name (e.g., if you enter just one or two letters, or even a space), it will search for any keyfields which contain these characters.

For example, imagine you have set up a file of information concerning various computers. Your keyfields would consist of names like "Timex Sinclair", "Commodore", "Apple", "Atari" etc.

Months later, when you want to examine the file, you will probably have forgotten whether your Timex Sinclair information is filed under "Timex Sinclair", "T/S", or "Timex". It doesn't matter: just enter "S" and then "T", and the routine will find it.

And is "Commodore" spelled with one or two m's? Who cares: just enter "Com".

But what if you enter "A"? Will the routine find "Apple" or "Atari"?

It will find which ever comes first, but it will also ask you to verify that it has located the correct record. So if it finds "Apple" and you wanted "Atari", just enter "n" and it will continue searching.

If the routine fails to find a match for your entry, the message "Record not found" appears, and you are asked to enter another.

TIP: It is advisable to ensure that *all* your keyfields contain at least one common character, e.g., a space or a full stop. Then, if you enter this character in response to the locate-a-record inquiry, it will find every record in turn, thus acting as a directory for your database.

LOCATE A RECORD

```
8500 LET n=10: DIM a$(n,15,15): FOR j=1 TO n: INPUT a$(j,1):
     NEXT j
8510 INPUT "Name of record ";t$
8520 IF t$="" THEN GO TO 8510
8530 FOR j=1 TO n
8540 FOR k=1 TO 15-LEN t$
8550 IF a$(j,1,k TO k+LEN t$-1)=t$ THEN GO TO 8600
8560 NEXT k: NEXT j
8570 PRINT FLASH 1;"RECORD NOT FOUND": GO TO 8510
8600 PRINT "FOUND ";a$(j,1)
8610 INPUT "Correct (Y/N) ? ";q$
8620 IF q$="n" THEN GO TO 8560
8630 IF q$="y" THEN RETURN
8640 GO TO 8610
9000 SAVE "LOCATE" LINE 0
```

8

Art for Art's Sake

- MARILYN
- PAINTING BY NUMBERS
- STARS AND STRIPES
- TUNE 1 AND 2

MARILYN

This program may take quite a while to key-in, but it is well worth the effort. It is a superb demonstration of Sinclair color graphics—not a line drawing or caricature, but a complete full color screen portrait.

And I do mean Sinclair graphics—the picture is composed entirely of the eight standard graphics characters; there are no high resolution plots or User Defined Graphics.

Only eight graphic characters? True, CHR$ 128 to CHR$ 143 all represent graphics, but eight of these are merely the *inverse* of the others. As the program defines PAPER and INK colors for each character, the concept or *inverse* has no meaning, and so CHR$ 136 to CHR$ 143 are not needed. (In fact, CHR$ 128 is not needed either, it being exactly the same as SPACE, CHR$ 32, so the picture only really uses *seven* graphics characters, plus *space*).

The first stage in the creation of the program was that the portrait was drawn onto graph paper. Transferring this to the screen required two further operations:

a. Setting up an array containing the relevant graphic characters.
b. Adding the colors by POKEing the attributes file.

The Array

There are 704 character positions on the screen, so a$() is a 704 element array, each element corresponding to a particular screen position. In other words when it is printed, a$(32) is the top right hand corner of the screen, a$(352) is somewhere in the middle.

There is no reason why you should not initialize a$ by defining a character for all 704 of its elements: your program would be very long but you could always use the two program technique (see "Fort-Data" and "Fortress") if you run short of memory. However there are short cuts.

You will probably find that most characters of a drawing are whole squares, i.e. CHR$ 128 or CHR$ 143. Not only are these characters exactly the same (with INK and PAPER colors reversed), they are also exactly the same as CHR$ 32 which is the default character put into every element of a$ when it is DIMensioned. The only characters which need be inserted into the array are the incomplete squares.

In writing this program, I first wrote down the numbers 129 to 135, and then counted through the squares of the graph paper drawing from 1 to 704. Each time a graphic character, other than a whole square, was encountered, I wrote down this alongside the appropriate character code.

This list became DATA lines 129 to 135 of the program, and lines 10 to 80 were added to READ the data into a$ and print it on the screen.

```
MARILYN

1 BORDER 1: CLS
5 LET x=9999
10 DIM a$(704)
20 FOR j=129 TO 135
30 RESTORE j
40 READ a: IF a=x THEN GO TO 70
50 LET a$(a)=CHR$ j
60 GO TO 40
70 NEXT j
80 PRINT a$
129 DATA 57,165,306,331,332,356,371,456,527,553,555,588,
        597,617,618,651,x
130 DATA 197,202,232,308,336,340,361,367,373,428,460,462,
        467,559,560,563,595,657,687,x
131 DATA 81,82,106,109,111,266,267,272,273,274,275,297,
        298,299,307,330,525,526,589,590,684,685,686,x
132 DATA 110,303,304,329,337,389,469,523,524,564,594,625,
        626,655,x
133 DATA 37,122,137,149,154,181,213,218,228,245,260,264,
        282,296,328,333,346,359,365,391,397,404,410,423,
        424,453,474,501,518,520,521,531,538,551,584,596,
        600,616,628,630,631,649,650,660,682,692,x
134 DATA 265,335,656,x
135 DATA 24,84,117,170,300,338,461,463,497,499,556,x
500 LET k=0: LET u=8: LET m=24: LET g=32: LET c=40:
        LET y=48: LET w=56
510 LET cy=46: LET yc=53
520 LET my=30: LET ym=51
530 LET mw=31: LET wm=59
540 LET yw=55: LET wy=62
550 LET mr=26: LET rm=19
560 LET wr=58: LET rw=23
570 LET gy=38: LET gm=35: LET wg=60: LET cw=47: LET kw=7:
        LET kg=4: LET km=3
1000 RESTORE 5000: FOR j=22528 TO 23231: READ a,b
1010 FOR k=1 TO b: POKE j,a: LET j=j+1: NEXT k: LET j=j-1
1020 NEXT j
1030 IF INKEY$<>"s" THEN GO TO 1030
1040 SAVE "MARILYN"SCREEN$
1050 STOP
```

[continued]

```
5000 DATA c,5,y,18,yc,1,c,12
5001 DATA cy,1,y,19,yc,1,c,11
5002 DATA y,12,my,2,m,1,my,1,y,5,c,11
5003 DATA y,5,my,1,m,2,my,1,ym,1,my,1,m,5,my,1,y,4,yc,1,c,10
5004 DATA y,4,ym,1,m,11,mw,1,y,4,yc,1,c,10
5005 DATA cy,1,y,4,ym,1,m,10,mw,1,y,4,c,11
5006 DATA yc,1,y,4,my,1,m,10,mw,1,y,4,yc,1,c,9
5007 DATA cy,1,y,3,wy,1,m,12,mw,1,y,5,c,9
5008 DATA cy,1,y,3,wm,1,km,1,m,1,km,1,m,4,km,1,m,2,km,1,
     m,1,w,1,y,4,yc,1,c,9
5009 DATA y,4,w,1,km,1,gm,2,km,1,m,2,mw,1,wg,1,g,1,gm,2,
     w,2,y,4,c,10
5010 DATA y,4,w,1,kw,1,u,1,kg,1,g,1,wm,1,m,1,wm,1,kg,1,
     kw,1,u,1,k,1,w,2,y,4,yc,1,c,9
5011 DATA cy,1,y,2,yw,1,m,5,wm,1,m,1,mw,1,m,5,wm,1,y,5,c,10
5012 DATA cy,1,y,1,yw,1,m,5,wm,1,m,6,mw,1,w,1,y,4,yc,1,c,10
5013 DATA y,2,yw,1,wm,1,m,3,wm,1,m,7,w,2,y,5,c,10
5014 DATA cy,1,y,2,wm,1,m,3,kw,4,m,3,wm,1,w,1,wy,1,y,4,yc,1,
     c,11
5015 DATA y,2,w,1,m,8,km,1,m,1,mw,1,w,1,wy,1,y,4,c,12
5016 DATA cy,1,y,1,yw,1,wm,1,m,1,mr,1,rw,1,rm,1,wr,1,rm,1,
     m,3,mw,1,w,1,y,5,yc,1,c,12
5017 DATA cy,1,y,1,wm,1,m,1,mr,1,rw,1,w,2,rw,1,mr,1,m,2,
     wm,1,wg,1,y,5,c,14
5018 DATA cy,1,w,1,m,2,mr,3,m,3,mw,2,wg,1,gy,1,y,2,yc,1,c,15
5019 DATA cy,1,yw,1,wm,1,m,6,mw,1,wm,1,m,1,wg,1,g,1,gy,1,
     yc,1,c,17
5020 DATA cy,1,yw,1,wm,1,m,3,mw,1,wm,1,mw,1,m,2,wg,1,g,2,c,19
5021 DATA cw,1,m,1,mw,4,m,4,wg,1,g,2,c,10
9000 SAVE "MARILYN" LINE 0
```

The Attributes

The next stage was to read through the graph paper drawing again, this time looking at the colors in each square.

Again you could use 704 statements to POKE each color combination into the Attributes file, but again there are short cuts.

Very often you will find that there are large blocks of color in your drawing, so it is easier to list the attributes of one square, followed by the number of squares for which these same attributes persist.

DATA lines 5000 to 5021 represent the attributes of the entire screen using this method. Notice that variable names are used in place of the actual attribute values. Lines 500 to 570, declaring the values of these variables, were added later, by consulting the program "ATTR Table".

Finally, lines 1000 to 1021 were added to READ the attributes data into the Attributes file, and the screen drawing was complete.

As with all the programs in Art for Art's Sake, "Marilyn" is intended as a demonstration, but once you have mastered the techniques, try creating your own Timex Sinclair portrait gallery.

Line 1040 allows you to save the picture *without* the program which created it (use LOAD "MARILYN"SCREEN$ to reproduce the picture at any time), or you can use the machine code routine "Pages" to store it for instant recall.

PAINTING BY NUMBERS

This is a much simpler program than "Marilyn"—the picture is created without using the Display file at all. It is composed entirely of "blanks," but because the blanks have a different PAPER color, the illusion of a picture is created! (If you don't believe that the picture is an illusion, try to copy it onto the T/S printer).

All you have to do is press the number key corresponding to the color you want to paint.

The BEEP tells you when the program is ready for another key press.

```
PAINTING BY NUMBERS

1 CLS : PRINT "55555775555555555555555565555556"
2 PRINT "55557775555555555557777556566565"
3 PRINT "22222777775555555557777555666655"
4 PRINT "66666277755577755557755666666666"
5 PRINT "44444625555777755555555555666655"
6 PRINT "11111462577777555555555556566565"
7 PRINT "33333146255775445555775565555556"
8 PRINT "55555314625555424477777655555445"
9 PRINT "55424531462555544244777755544244"
10 PRINT "54444553146254454445427755554442"
11 PRINT "44245555314624240504244555545244"
12 PRINT "24444555314625445054445542444050"
13 PRINT "44454455314625555055555554424405"
14 PRINT "05044245314625555055555445444204"
15 PRINT "50544444314625555055555444050405"
16 PRINT "50552555314625555055555525505505"
17 PRINT "40444444444444444404444444404404"
18 PRINT "40444444444444444404444444404404"
19 PRINT "40444441111114444444444444404404"
20 PRINT "40444111111111111444444444404444"
21 PRINT "40441111111111111111444444404444"
22 PRINT "40111111111111111111114444404444"
50 LET a$="01234567"
100 BEEP .1,20
105 LET i$=INKEY$: IF i$="*" THEN GO TO 105
110 FOR p=1 TO 8: IF i$=a$(p) THEN GO TO 120
115 NEXT p: GO TO 105
120 BEEP .1,50: FOR j=0 TO 21: FOR k=0 TO 31
125 IF SCREEN$ (j,k)=i$ THEN PRINT AT j,k; PAPER
      VAL i$;CHR$ 32
130 NEXT k: NEXT j
135 LET a$(p)="*": IF a$="********" THEN STOP
140 GO TO 100
9000 SAVE "PAINTING" LINE 0
```

STARS AND STRIPES

You are faced with an immediate mathematical problem when attempting to draw the American flag on the Timex Sinclair screen. The stars section of the flag is nine characters deep (assuming that you are using the asterisk character as a star, which seems logical). But adjacent to these nine characters there are only seven rows of stripes, and seven into nine just does not go.

You must therefore think in terms of pixels rather than characters. The stars reach a depth of 9 × 8=72 pixels; all right so seven into seventy-two does not go either, but it is a lot less objectionable to make one stripe two pixels deeper than the others than it is to have two extra stripes in the flag.

So, the top stripe is 12 pixels deep, and all the others are 10 pixels. You could create them using PLOT and DRAW statements, but I have chosen to use the normal Timex Sinclair graphics, plus two User Defined Graphics (CHR$ 144 = 6 rows of PAPER pixels and 2 of INK; CHR$ 145= 2 rows of PAPER and 6 of INK).

The DATA for the User Defined Graphics is in line 500. DATA line 1000 contains the CODEs of the characters used to print the stripes.

```
STARS & STRIPES

5 BORDER 0: PAPER 7: CLS
10 RESTORE : FOR j=USR CHR$ 144 TO USR CHR$ 144+15:
        READ a: POKE j,a: NEXT j
15 LET s$="* * * * * *": REM spaces between asterisks
20 LET t$=" "+s$( TO 10)
25 PRINT PAPER 1; INK 7;s$'t$'s$'t$'s$'t$'s$'t$'s$
30 DIM b$(5)
35 FOR j=0 TO 16: READ a
40 FOR k=11*(j<=9) TO 26: PRINT PAPER 7*(j<16); INK 2;
        AT j,k;CHR$ a;: NEXT k: PRINT PAPER 0;b$
45 NEXT j: DIM b$(32)
50 FOR j=0 TO 4: PRINT PAPER 0;b$: NEXT j
60 GO TO 60
500 DATA 0,0,0,0,0,0,255,255,0,0,255,255,255,255,255,255
1000 DATA 143,131,144,143,128,145,131,144,143,128,145,131,
        144,143,128,145,131
9000 SAVE "FLAG" LINE 0
```

TUNES 1 AND 2

There is a joke in the English Timex Sinclair manual (at least I hope it is a joke) where they ask you to write a program to play the whole of the Mahler's first symphony.

That is a pretty formidable task, especially if you have to enter every single note as a separate BEEP statement, which is the method the manual uses.

It would be slightly easier if you used DATA statements to specify the duration and pitch of each BEEP, as in "Tune 1."

"Tune 2" uses SEPARATE DATA statements to hold duration (lines 100—) and pitch (lines 200—), and the data is read into arrays before the tune is played.

This method may seem clumsy, but it makes composing very much simpler; you can decide on the pitch of the notes first, and add the duration later.

Incidentally, neither of these tunes is by Mahler, but, with luck, you may recognize them. (At least, if you are as old as me, you may recognize them.)

```
TUNE 1

5 RESTORE
10 READ p,d: BEEP d/5,p: GO TO 10
100 DATA 12,2,12,2,9,3,9,1,9,2,5,2,0,2,2,2,5,2,5,2,9,9
110 DATA 9,1,9,1,9,1,9,2,5,2,5,2,2,2,0,2,0,1,0,1,2,2,5,3,
       7,1,5,10
120 DATA 12,2,12,2,9,2,10,2,9,2,5,2,0,1,0,1,2,1,5,3,5,2,
       7,10
130 DATA 5,2,5,4,2,1,2,1,2,2,0,2,5,2,5,3,2,1,2,2,0,4,2,2,
       5,2,7,2,5,18
9000 SAVE "TUNE 1" LINE 0
```

TUNE 2

```
5 DIM p(65): DIM d(65)
10 RESTORE 100: FOR j=1 TO 65: READ p(j): NEXT j
15 RESTORE 200: FOR j=1 TO 65: READ d(j): NEXT j
20 FOR k=1 TO 5: FOR j=1 TO 65
25 BEEP d(j)/5,p(j)
30 NEXT j
35 PAUSE 20: NEXT k: STOP
100 DATA 7,7,7,7,7,7,7,9,7,9,11
110 DATA 14,14,14,14,14,14,12,11,9,9,9,9
120 DATA 7,7,7,7,7,7,7,7,9,7,9,11
130 DATA 14,14,14,14,14,12,11,9,9
140 DATA 14,14,14,14,14,14,14,14,14,14,14,14,14
150 DATA 11,12,14,14,12,11,9,7
200 DATA 2,1,3,2,1,3,2,1,3,2,10
210 DATA 1,1,2,2,2,1,3,2,2,2,2,2
220 DATA 2,2,2,2,2,3,1,2,4,1,1,10
230 DATA 1,1,4,2,2,2,2,2,8
240 DATA 1,1,1,3,2,1,1,2,2,2,2,2,4
250 DATA 1,1,6,2,2,2,12,8
9000 SAVE "TUNE 2" LINE 0
```

9

Under the Spreading Chestnut Tree

- BULLS AND COWS
- HANGDATA/HANGMAN
- HANGMAN
- SIMON SAYS
- SKETCHPAD

BULLS AND COWS

The programs in this section are almost as old as computers themselves, and they are all based on precomputer ideas which have been around since the beginning of time. If I saw a book which included these programs I would say, "Oh no, hasn't this writer got any imagination at all." Of course, if everybody felt this way, then nobody would ever publish these programs, and they would become so rare that everybody would want to publish them.

But while the program ideas are as old as the hills, the programs themselves are all newly written especially for the Timex Sinclair. Furthermore, they are all examples of how I have approached these particular ideas; different programs may have achieved similar results by using totally different approaches.

"Bulls and Cows" is the old code-breaker game, which is also known by countless other names. The Timex Sinclair creates a code consisting of any four of the six colors (excluding black and white). Duplicate colors are allowed.

You have ten "guesses" in which to break the code. Use the keys 1 to 6 corresponding to the six colors, to enter your "guess."

The Timex Sinclair marks each "guess" by awarding you a black mark for each correct color in the correct position, and a white mark for each correct color in an incorrect position.

Notice I have used the word "guess" in quotes. This is purely a game of skill; all your previous guesses and marks remain on screen, so you should always be able to deduce the code in less than 10 guesses. In fact the game has been extensively analysed and it has been proved to be possible to crack *any* code in not more than 5 guesses.

BULLS & COWS

```
5 RESTORE: FOR j=0 TO 7: READ p: POKE USR CHR$ 144+j,p:
       NEXT j
10  BORDER 7: PAPER 7: INK 9: CLS
20 DIM a(4): DIM b(4): DIM c(4)
30 LET s=1: RANDOMIZE
40 FOR j=1 TO 4: LET a(j)=INT (RND*6)+1: NEXT j
50 PRINT s; TAB 3;
60 FOR j=1 TO 4
70 LET i$=INKEY$
80 IF i$<"1" OR i$>"6" THEN GO TO 70
90 PRINT INK VAL i$;CHR$ 143;CHR$ 32;CHR$ 32;
100 IF i$=INKEY$ THEN GO TO 100
110 LET b(j)=VAL i$: LET c(j)=a(j)
120 NEXT j: PRINT CHR$ 32;CHR$ 32;
130 LET p=0
140 FOR j=1 TO 4
150 IF b(j)=c(j) THEN GO SUB 500
160 NEXT j
170 IF p=4 THEN GO TO 700
180 FOR j=1 TO 4: FOR h=1 TO 4
190 IF b(j)>0 AND b(j)=c(h) THEN GO SUB 600
200 NEXT h: NEXT j
210 PRINT: PRINT
220 IF NOT p THEN BEEP .5,2: GO TO 240
230 FOR j=p TO 3: BEEP .1,5: NEXT j
240 LET s=s+1: IF s<=10 THEN GO TO 50
300 PRINT "You have failed to break code:-"
310 PRINT TAB 3;: FOR j=1 TO 4: PRINT INK a(j);CHR$ 143;
       CHR$ 32;CHR$ 32;: NEXT j
320 INPUT "P to play again: X to stop ";a$
330 IF a$="p" THEN RUN
340 IF a$="x" THEN STOP
350 GO TO 320
500 PRINT CHR$ 143;CHR$ 32;: BEEP .01,50: LET b(j)=0:
       LET c(j)=0: LET p=p+1: RETURN
600 PRINT CHR$ 144;CHR$ 32;: BEEP .01,30: LET b(j)=0:
       LET c(h)=0: LET p=p+1: RETURN
700 PRINT AT s*2,9; INK 2; FLASH 1;"CORRECT IN ";s
710 GO TO 320
1000 DATA 255,129,129,129,129,129,129,255
9000 SAVE "B&C" LINE 0
```

HANGDATA/HANGMAN

Don't try and tell me that you haven't got a Hangman program already. There seems to be one in every computer book you look at.

The main difference is that this version also employs a data-file of words, so that you can play the game for a considerable length of time without employing a second person to enter another word for you to guess.

"Hangdata" is the data-file set up program. You can enter as many words as you like, the only constraints being the Timex Sinclair's memory size and your patience. I suspect that the latter of these will usually be the limiting factor.

Words should not be more than 32 characters long, but may include spaces, hyphens, or, if you want to be really evil, even graphics characters.

To avoid problems caused by upper and lower case letters, however, "Hangdata" includes a routine (line 70) to convert lower to upper case. "Hangman" also includes similar routines (lines 110 and 180).

Once you have entered your words, they are saved on tape, to be loaded automatically by the "Hangman" program.

Ideally, therefore, your "Hangman" tape should contain a copy of "Hangman," followed immediately by a data-file created by "Hangdata." However, there is no limit to the number of data-files you can create, and it is a good idea to build up a library of data-files containing various levels of difficulty for different age groups.

```
HANGDATA

10 PRINT "How many words do you want to"'"enter?"
20 INPUT n: CLS
30 DIM w$(n+1,33): LET w$(1)=STR$ n
40 FOR j=2 TO n+1
50 INPUT ("Enter word #";j-1;":");t$
60 LET l=LEN t$: IF NOT l OR l>32 THEN GO TO 50
70 FOR k=1 TO l: IF t$(k)>="a" AND t$(k)<="z" THEN LET
       t$(k)=CHR$ (CODE t$(k)-32)
80 IF t$(k)<CHR$ 32 THEN GO TO 50
90 NEXT k
100 LET w$(j)=CHR$ l+t$
110 PRINT t$: NEXT j
120 SAVE "data" DATA w$()
130 STOP
9000 CLEAR : SAVE "HANGDATA" LINE 0
```

HANGMAN

This version sticks so closely to the original pencil and paper version that few words of explanation are necessary.

The man and gallows are drawn line by line, and you are dead when the drawing is complete. (11 incorrect guesses).

The two data statements (lines 1000 and 1010) contain the PLOT and DRAW coordinates for the hangman drawing. There are two PLOT and two DRAW coordinates for each line, except for the head, which (surprise, surprise), is drawn by the CIRCLE statement in line 2000.

If you fail to guess the word, the missing letters are flashed on screen (lines 510 to 530).

When you have used up all the words, you may either:

Enter RUN to load a new data-file

or

Enter GO TO 10 to repeat the same words (in a different order).

```
HANGMAN

5 LOAD "data" DATA w$()
10 BORDER 4: PAPER 4: INK 9
15 LET n=VAL w$(1)
20 DIM w(n): LET u=1
25 CLS : RESTORE
30 IF INKEY$="p" OR INKEY$="P" THEN GO TO 30
35 LET w=INT (RND*n)+2
40 FOR j=1 TO u: IF w(j)=w THEN GO TO 35
45 NEXT j: LET w(u)=w: LET u=u+1
50 LET t$=w$(w,2 TO CODE w$(w,1)+1): LET l=LEN t$
55 FOR j=1 TO l: PRINT AT 0,j;CHR$ 45: NEXT j: LET j=0
60 LET r=0
100 LET i$=INKEY$: IF i$<CHR$ 32 THEN GO TO 100
110 IF i$>="a" AND i$<="z" THEN LET i$=CHR$ (CODE i$-32)
120 LET x=1: FOR k=1 TO l
130 IF t$(k)=i$ THEN PRINT AT 0,k;i$: LET x=0: LET t$(k)=
        CHR$ 0: LET r=r+1
140 NEXT k
150 IF x THEN LET j=j+1: GO SUB 2000
160 IF j=11 THEN GO TO 500
170 IF r=l THEN GO TO 600
180 IF INKEY$=i$ OR INKEY$=CHR$ (CODE i$+32) THEN
        GO TO 180
190 GO TO 100
```

[continued]

```
500 PRINT AT 15,15; FLASH 1; INK 2; PAPER 7;"FAILURE"
510 FOR k=1 TO l
520 IF t$(k)<>CHR$ 0 THEN PRINT AT 0,k; FLASH 1; INK 2;
      PAPER 7; t$(k)
530 NEXT k
540 IF u=n+1 THEN PRINT AT 21,2;"ALL WORDS HAVE BEEN USED":
      GO TO 9999
550 PRINT AT 21,0;"PRESS P TO PLAY AGAIN: X TO STOP"
560 IF INKEY$="p" OR INKEY$="P" THEN GO TO 25
570 IF INKEY$="x" OR INKEY$="X" THEN GO TO 9999
580 GO TO 560
600 PRINT AT 15,15; FLASH 1; INK 2; PAPER 7;"SUCCESS"
610 GO TO 540
1000 DATA 16,40,48,0,40,40,0,72,40,112,24,0,64,112,0,-10,
      40,100,12,12
1010 DATA 64,96,6,64,90,0,-24,64,66,-8,-12,64,66,8,-12,64,
      82,-12,2,64,82,12,2
2000 READ a,b: IF j=6 THEN READ c: CIRCLE a,b,c: GO TO
      2020
2010 PLOT a,b: READ c,d: DRAW c,d
2020 RETURN
9000 CLEAR : SAVE "HANGMAN" LINE 0
9999 STOP
```

SIMON SAYS

In the traditional version of Simon Says, you had to repeat everything that Simon did, which could lead to some very bizarre situations.

The computer version is a lot more dignified. Simon (Timex Sinclair) gives an ever-lengthening sequence of colors, and you must repeat the sequence (using the color keys 0 to 7).

Each color has an associated tone, and the color is flashed on screen in a position corresponding to its keyboard position, so if you want to make the game really difficult, try playing it on a black and white television (my best score this way is 4).

On a color television, of course, it is possible to achieve much higher scores. However, the game is more than a simple test of memory because, as the sequence lengthens, the speed increases dramatically.

Subroutine 1000 flashes the colors and makes the BEEP.

The time variable, t, varies inversely with the length of the sequence.

If (when) you make an error, line 510 repeats the sequence, after setting t to a constant 0.8 seconds, and calling the subroutine at line 1005 instead of line 1000.

```
SIMON SAYS

5 BORDER 7: PAPER 7: INK 9: BRIGHT 0: CLS : DIM b$(32)
10 RANDOMIZE
15 LET r$=""
20 LET x=INT (RND*8)
25 LET r$=r$+STR$ x
30 LET n=LEN r$
35 FOR j=1 TO n
40 LET x=VAL r$(j)
45 GO SUB 1000
50 NEXT j
100 PRINT AT 20,0;"NOW YOU REPEAT THE SEQUENCE"
105 FOR j=1 TO n
110 LET i$=INKEY$
115 IF i$<"0" OR i$>"7" THEN GO TO 110
120 LET x=VAL i$
125 GO SUB 1000
130 IF INKEY$=i$ THEN GO TO 130
135 IF i$<>r$(j) THEN GO TO 500
140 NEXT j
145 PRINT AT 20,0;b$;AT 20,0;"Total so far: ";n
150 FOR j=1 TO 100: NEXT j
155 CLS : GO TO 20
500 PRINT AT 20,0; INK 9; FLASH 1;"ERROR!!!!! The sequence
        was"
505 FOR j=1 TO 250: NEXT j
510 LET t=.8: FOR j=1 TO n: LET x=VAL r$(j): GO SUB 1005:
        NEXT j
515 PRINT AT 20,0;b$;AT 20,0;"You scored ";n-1'"Press
        ""R"" to try again"
520 IF INKEY$<>"r" THEN GO TO 520
530 RUN
1000 LET t=1/n
1005 PRINT AT 6,x*3+30*(x=0); INK x; BRIGHT 1;CHR$ 143;:
        BEEP t,x*7+56*(x=0): PRINT CHR$ 8;CHR$ 32
1010 RETURN
9000 SAVE "SIMON SAYS" LINE 0
```

SKETCHPAD

Why people spend hundreds of dollars on a computer and then use it as a sketchpad, I will never know. Still, these programs are fun, and you can create some very good pictures with the Timex Sinclair's high resolution graphics.

In this program, a spot cursor indicates the current DRAW position. The arrow keys 5 to 8 will cause a line to be drawn in the appropriate direction.

You can move the cursor about, without drawing, by pressing key "1" which will cause the cursor to flash, and then using keys 5 to 8 as before. In this mode, the cursor will also pass through previously drawn lines without erasing them. To start drawing again, press key "0" to obtain the normal cursor.

To erase a line, press key "0" (you would think the Timex Sinclair was short of keys, the way I have given key "0" two completely different functions), and the direction keys will now undraw. Press key "0" again to return to the normal mode.

One interesting point to notice—this has nothing to do with "Sketchpad", but it just happens that this is the only program where I have used this technique.

If you put the operating instructions to a program into a REM statement at the end, you can LIST this line during the program (see line 1) and then continue. I do not know if this has any advantages over simply PRINTing the instructions, but it is something that most other computers will not do, so I had to use it somewhere.

SKETCHPAD

```
1 BORDER 7: INK 0: PAPER 7: CLS : LIST 9999
5 IF INKEY$<>"r" THEN GO TO 5
10 LET move=0: LET retain=0
15 PAPER 0: BORDER 0: INK 7: CLS
20 LET x1=0: LET y1=0
25 LET x=0: LET y=0
30 LET x1=x+x1: LET y1=y+y1
35 IF INKEY$="0" THEN LET move=NOT move: LET retain=0
40 IF INKEY$="1" THEN LET move=1: LET retain=1
45 IF INKEY$="0" THEN GO TO 45
50 LET x=((INKEY$="8")*(x1<255))-((INKEY$="5")*
        (x1>0))
55 LET y=((INKEY$="7")*(y1<175))-((INKEY$="6")*
        (y1>0))
60 IF retain=1 AND POINT (x1,y1)=1 THEN GO TO 30
65 PLOT OVER 0;x1,y1
70 IF move=1THEN PLOT OVER 1;x1,y1
75 GO TO 30
9000 SAVE "SKETCHPAD" LINE 0
9999 REM Use arrow keys to draw.
         Use key 1 to reposition
 cursor. Use key 0 to delete.
         Use key 0 to switch off
 delete/reposition functions.

       Press R to RUN
```

10

Play It Again Sam

- SKYLINE
- GAUNTLET
- FLYING SAUCERS
- FIREPOWER

SKYLINE

You are the commander of an alien space craft about to land on Earth. Choosing some large modern city like London or New York, in the over-optimistic belief that you might find some sort of intelligent life there, you make your approach. You fail completely to notice the perfectly good airfields in the vicinity, and head directly for the center of town.

The skyscrapers could present something of a problem but assuming them to be nothing but heaps of rubble (a natural enough mistake), you decide to do Earthlings a favor by flattening them and creating a new landing strip.

There are three ways in which you can destroy the skyscapers (one story at a time):

a) with bombs (key "0")
b) with missiles (key "9")
c) by crashing into a skyscraper with one of your ships.

This last method is not recommended, as you only have four ships with which to effect a successful landing.

The prime objective of the game is to flatten all the skyscrapers, thereby enabling one of your ships to land. Points are of secondary importance only. It is no use having a high score if all four of your ships have crashed. However, you cannot fire a missile unless you have a positive score.

Points are scored as follows:

1 for each story of a skyscraper destroyed by a bomb
–20 for using a missile
–20 for crashing a ship

Bonus points for a successful landing:

400 for landing ship number one
300 for landing ship number two, etc.

Bombs, therefore, are your most important weapon; they always fall vertically, but of course they can miss (which wastes time).

Missiles are expensive weapons, to be used in emergencies only (and then only if you have a positive score to enable you to use them). Missiles are fired horizontally, but they *never* miss. If there is not a skyscraper directly ahead of you, they will wrap around the screen until they eventually hit one. Your ship's descent is frozen while a missile is in the air, so you may sometimes use them to give yourself a few seconds breathing space to plan your strategy.

Program Notes

The four User Defined Graphics are:

```
CHR$ 144 & CHR$ 145: Your ship
CHR$ 146: Bomb
CHR$ 147: A skyscraper story
```

The skyline is created by lines 105 to 130. Array t$() holds the position of the individual skyscraper blocks, and as stories are destroyed the contents of the array are changed accordingly. The program does not PEEK the screen, which in any case is virtually impossible on the Timex Sinclair, or use ATTR or SCREEN$ to determine the presence of a skyscraper block, but merely compares the position of your ship/bomb/missile with the equivalent element of t$.

The main program loop (ship descent) is from line 200 to line 360 (or to line 250 while you are in the top half of the screen, above the top of the skyscrapers). Lines 365 to 390 represent a ship crash.

Subroutine 1000 prints the bomb position, with lines 1100 to 1115 indicating a hit.

Routine 2000 prints the missile position, in exactly the same way as the main ship descent loop, and it is not left until an eventual hit (line 2050). (Note: Line 2045 is a piece of idiot-proofing. There is obviously no need to waste points by firing a missile once all the skyscrapers have been destroyed, but in case anybody does, this line terminates the routine when the missile reaches the bottom right hand corner of the screen.)

Making the Game Easier/Harder

The density of the skyscrapers is controlled by the limit value of k in line 120. Having k=1 TO 3 will tend to make the skyline less dense; k=1 TO 5 will tend to make it more dense.

Line 225 prevents the bomb button from working every time when you are just about to land. This adds a little last minute panic to the game, as you may be forced to use missiles to destroy some of the bottom stories. If you find this too frustrating, you can delete the line completely.

To change the number of ships, change line 385. To change the scoring, see lines: 375 (crash); 1100 (bombs); 2005 (missiles); 5000 (bonus).

SKYLINE

```
1 DATA 0,255,127,255,106,255,127,255
2 DATA 0,192,240,252,191,252,240,192
3 DATA 42,62,28,62,62,62,28,8
4 DATA 255,255,195,195,195,195,255,255
5 DATA 0,0,132,198,255,198,132,0
10 FOR g=1 TO 5: RESTORE g
15 FOR j=0 TO 7
20 READ a: POKE USR CHR$ (g+143)+j,a
25 NEXT j
30 NEXT g
40 LET s$=CHR$ 32+CHR$ 144+CHR$ 145: LET b$=CHR$ 146
50 RANDOMIZE
100 BORDER 5: PAPER 0: INK 6: CLS
105 DIM t$(11,32)
110 FOR j=11 TO 21
115 IF j>11 THEN LET t$(j-10)=t$(j-11)
120 FOR k=1 TO 4: LET t$(j-10,(INT (RND*32)+1))=CHR$ 147:
       NEXT k
125 PRINT INK 7;AT j,0;t$(j-10)
130 NEXT j
135 PRINT AT 0,2; INK 7;"WEAPONS: 9=Missile   0=Bomb"
200 LET sc=0: LET sl=0
205 LET x=sl*2+2: LET y=0: LET bf=0
210 PRINT AT 1,0; INK 4;"SCORE:";sc,"SHIPS LOST:";sl
215 PRINT AT x,y;s$
220 IF INKEY$="0" AND bf=0 THEN LET bf=1: LET bx=x:
       LET by=y: BEEP .01,25
225 IF bf THEN IF x=20 THEN LET bf=INT (RND*2)
230 IF INKEY$="9" AND sc>0 THEN GO TO 2000
235 IF bf THEN GO SUB 1000
300 LET y=y+1
305 IF y=32 THEN LET y=0: LET x=x+1
310 IF x=21 AND y=30 THEN GO TO 5000
350 IF x<11 THEN GO TO 210
355 LET a=x-10: LET b=y+3: IF b>32 THEN LET b=b-32:
       LET a=a+1
360 IF t$(a,b)<>CHR$ 147 THEN GO TO 210
365 FOR k=7 TO 0 STEP-1: PRINT AT x,y; INK k;s$: BEEP .1,k:
       NEXT k
370 LET t$(a,b)=CHR$ 32
375 LET sl=sl+1: LET sc=sc-20
380 IF bf=1 THEN PRINT AT bx,by;CHR$ 32
385 IF sl=4 THEN GO TO 4000
390 GO TO 205
1000 PRINT AT bx,by;CHR$ 32
1005 IF bx=21 THEN GO TO 1030
1010 LET bx=bx+1
1015 IF bx<11 THEN GO TO 1025
1020 IF t$(bx-10,by+1)=CHR$ 147 THEN GO TO 1100
```

```
1025 PRINT INK 2;AT bx,by;b$
1030 IF bx=21 THEN BEEP .05,5: PRINT AT bx,by;CHR$ 32:
     LET bf=0
1040 RETURN
1100 LET sc=sc+1
1105 LET bf=0: LET t$(bx-10,by+1)=CHR$ 32: PRINT AT bx,by;
     CHR$ 32
1110 BEEP .01,35
1115 RETURN
2000 LET a=x: LET b=y+3: IF b>31 THEN LET b=b-32: LET a=a+1
2005 LET sc=sc-20
2010 IF a>=11 THEN GO TO 2040
2015 PRINT AT x,y; INK 1+(b/2=INT (b/2));s$
2020 PRINT AT a,b; INK 3;CHR$ 148
2025 BEEP .01,40
2030 PRINT AT a,b;CHR$ 32
2035 LET b=b+1: IF b=32 THEN LET b=0: LET a=a+1
2040 IF a<11 THEN GO TO 2015
2045 IF t$(a-10,b+1)=CHR$ 147 THEN LET t$(a-10,b+1)=CHR$ 32:
     PRINT AT a,b;CHR$ 32: BEEP 1,35: GO TO 210
2050 IF a=21 AND b=31 THEN GO TO 210
2055 GO TO 2015
4000 PRINT AT 10,10; INK 2; PAPER 7; FLASH 1;"ALL SHIPS LOST"
4005 GO TO 5010
5000 PRINT AT 10,13; INK 2; PAPER 7; FLASH 1;"SUCCESS":
     LET sc=sc+100*(4-sl)
5005 PRINT AT 1,0; INK 8; PAPER 8; FLASH 1;"SCORE ";sc
5010 PRINT AT 15,5; PAPER 7; INK 2;"Press ""P"" to play
     again";AT 17,10;"or ""X"" to stop"
5015 IF INKEY$="x" THEN GO TO 5030
5020 IF INKEY$="p" THEN RUN 40
5025 GO TO 5015
5030 PAPER 5: INK 0: CLS : PRINT AT 10,15;"BYE": STOP
9000 SAVE "SKYLINE" LINE 0
```

GAUNTLET

"Gauntlet" is what I call a "War Game for Pacifists." You are under constant attack but you yourself are unable to attack the enemy in any way. You must try to avoid defeat merely by using your various defense mechanisms.

Your space ship starts at the top left of the screen and travels to and fro until finally it lands at the bottom left of the screen. (Note the reverse of direction in this game, as opposed to the wrap-around of "Skyline.")

The bad guys operate the laser guns at the bottom of the screen. Being hit by a laser does not, in itself, destroy your ship, but it does deplete your energy reserves, which are the key to this game. You start with 1000 energy units, and these are used up one by one as you cross the screen. You can collect additional units at the green cross stations at various points on your descent, so if you can avoid the laser beams you should be able to land safely.

Defense Mechanisms

The following mechanisms will all afford you a certain degree of protection against the lasers, *but* they all consume energy;

Key	Energy cost	Effect
0	5 units	Reduces the effective RANGE of the lasers.
9	10 units	Reduces the FREQUENCY of laser shots.
8	20 units	Increases the speed of your ships.

Program Notes

The program uses two User Defined Graphics, one for a ship traveling to the right, one for a ship traveling to the left.

The rapid laser shots are produced by the DRAW commands in subroutine 1000.

A hit is deleted by the ATTR function in line 1015. The ship is drawn in INK 6, the laser beam in INK 2. Therefore the laser beam will change the attributes of the ship's position from 6 to 2 if there is a hit.

The length of each laser is determined by variable 1, (normally 144 pixels, but reduced when INKEY$="0", line 60)

The laser to be fired is determined by the random number x (line 1000), and when x exceeds 6, no shot is fired. The random number is in the range 1 to t, so the higher the value of t, the smaller the possibility of a shot. The variable t is initially set to 7, for *almost* constant firing, and is increased when INKEY$="9", line 55.

GAUNTLET

```
1 RESTORE: FOR j=0 TO 23: READ a: POKE USR (CHR$ 144)+j, a:
       NEXT j
5 BORDER 0: PAPER 0: INK 7: CLS
10 RANDOMIZE
15 LET e=1000: PRINT "ENERGY LEFT ";e
20 LET a=2: LET b=0
25 FOR j=3 TO 18 STEP 3: PRINT AT j,0; INK 4;CHR$ 146;
       AT j,31; INK 4;CHR$ 146; AT 21,4*j/3; INK 3;
       "↑": NEXT j
35 LET s$=CHR$ (144+(a/2<>INT (a/2)))
40 IF e<0 THEN LET e=0
45 PRINT AT 0,12;e;CHR$ 32;CHR$ 32: IF e=0 THEN GO TO 500
50 PRINT AT a,b; INK 6;s$
55 LET t=7: IF INKEY$="9" THEN LET e=e-10: LET t=4*t+RND*10
60 LET l=144: IF INKEY$="0" THEN LET e=e-5: LET l=
       INT (RND*144)+1
65 GO SUB 1000
70 LET an=a: LET bn=b
75 IF INKEY$="8" THEN LET e=e-20: LET bn=bn-2+4*(s$=CHR$ 144)
80 LET bn=bn-1+2*(s$=CHR$ 144): IF bn>31 OR bn<0 THEN
       LET an=an+1: LET bn=31*(s$=CHR$ 144): IF an=20
       THEN GO TO 550
85 PRINT AT a,b;CHR$ 32
90 LET e=e-1: IF ATTR (an,bn)=4 THEN LET e=e+INT (RND*100)
       +75: BEEP .1,55
100 LET a=an: LET b=bn: GO TO 35
500 PRINT AT 3,9; INK 2; FLASH 1;"SHIP DESTROYED"
510 FOR j=7 TO 0 STEP -1: PRINT AT a,b; INK j; BRIGHT 1;
       "*": BEEP .5,j*8: NEXT j
520 GO TO 600
550 PRINT AT 3,1; INK 4; FLASH 1;"YOU LANDED SAFELY. WELL
       DONE"
600 INPUT "Enter P to play : X to stop ";s$
610 IF s$="p" THEN RUN 15
620 IF s$="x" THEN GO TO 9999
630 GO TO 600
1000 LET x=INT (RND*t)+1: IF x>6 THEN PAUSE 5: RETURN
1005 LET x=32*x+4
1010 PLOT INK 2;x,9
1015 LET c=0: DRAW OVER 1; INK 2;0,l: IF ATTR (a,b)<>6
       THEN LET c=1
1020 BEEP .01,l/3
1025 IF c THEN PRINT FLASH 1; PAPER 2;AT a,b;"*": BEEP 1,20:
       LET e=e-INT (RND*50)-100
1030 PLOT OVER 1; INK 2;x,9: DRAW OVER 1; INK 2;0,l
1035 RETURN
5000 DATA 0,224,112,255,112,224,0,0,0,7,14,255,14,7,0,0,
       60,60,255,255,255,255,60,60
9000 SAVE "GAUNTLET" LINE 0
9999 STOP
```

FLYING SAUCERS

In "Skyline" you had all the weapons and the defenders had none. In "Gauntlet" the defenders had them all, and *you* had none. Isn't it about time for a more evenly matched contest?

In this game, you operate the missile bases on the ground, but instead of flying passively overhead, the enemy flying saucers hurl bombs at you constantly. What is more, while your shots must be fired vertically upward, the saucers have the annoying ability to aim diagonally in your direction. They also use invisible saucers from time to time, which are not easy to hit but which can earn you bonus points. Oh, and just to make it difficult, the rings of the saucers are ethereal; you must make a direct hit on the body of the saucer to score. Your base, on the other hand, is very vulnerable, and you can easily run sideways into bombs which would otherwise have missed.

Your control keys are "8" and "9" to move left and right, and "0" to fire. The game is over when 50 saucers have successfully passed overhead, and of course you win if, by that time, you have scored more hits than them. You should not despair if you are miles behind with only a few saucers to go. Every time you score a hit, the saucer count is not incremented, and a new saucer is launched on the same flightpath as the one you have just hit. Thus it is possible, with skill, to get into a rhythm and score a large number of hits before a saucer makes a successful pass.

Program Notes

The User Defined Graphics are:

CHR$ 144: Missile base

CHR$ 145 & CHR$ 146: Flying saucer.

The main program loop is from line 1015 to line 1055. Saucers are launched at coordinates a,b which are both randomly determined in line 1005.

The color (INK) of the saucers is also random, and is largely irrelevant, *except* that blue INK on blue PAPER will create the invisible saucers.

Subroutine 100 (called twice in the main loop—remember this from "Practice Game") moves the missile base.

Subroutine 100 prints new stars (see below).

Subroutine 5000 prints your missiles.

Subroutine 6000 prints the bombs.

Strategy

The stars in this game are very important, and are more than just a pretty backdrop for the action.

You cannot have more than one missile in the air at any one time, so time is wasted while you wait for a missile to either hit something or to reach the top of the screen. Stars act as useful targets, in that they will destroy your wayward missiles, allowing you another shot. (Hitting a star does not, of course, score any points, and the star itself is also destroyed.) On the other hand, stars between you and the saucers will prevent you from getting a clear shot at your real target. Strategic play should therefore entail endeavoring to retain a blanket of stars in the upper sky, and destroying those nearer the ground. Often it is worth spending the early part of the game ignoring the saucers (but avoiding their bombs) and simply trying to create a favorable star pattern.

However, the stars have no effect on the enemy, and both saucers and bombs can pass them with impunity. They do destroy the stars they pass, however, which *may* work to your advantage. Also, remember that up to ten new stars are formed each time a saucer is launched.

```
FLYING SAUCERS

1 RESTORE: FOR j=USR CHR$ 144 TO USR CHR$ 144+23:
        READ a: POKE j,a: NEXT j
5 BORDER 1: PAPER 1: INK 0: CLS
10 FOR k=1 TO 10: GO SUB 8500: NEXT k
15 LET s$=CHR$ 32+CHR$ 145+CHR$ 146
20 LET bf=0: LET mf=0: LET h=0: LET x=15: LET s=0:
LET t=0: LET ns=0
25 PRINT AT 0,0; PAPER 5;"YOU";TAB 8;"SAUCERS LAUNCHED";
        TAB 28;"THEM"'s;TAB 15;ns;TAB 31;t
30 GO SUB 8600: GO TO 1000
100 LET x1=x+(INKEY$="9" AND x<31)-(INKEY$="8" AND x>0)
110 IF x<>x1 THEN PRINT AT 21,x;CHR$ 32;AT 21,x1; INK 6;
        CHR$ 144: LET x=x1
120 IF INKEY$="0" AND mf=0 THEN LET mf=1
130 RETURN
1000 GO SUB 8500
```

[continued]

```
1005 LET a=INT (RND*10): LET b=INT (RND*10): LET a=17-a:
     LET i=INT (RND*7)+1
1010 LET ns=ns+1: PRINT AT 1,15; PAPER 8;ns: IF ns>50
     THEN GO TO 7000
1015 IF bf=0 THEN LET bf=1: LET bx=a+1: LET y=SGN (x-b):
     LET by=b+y
1020 IF h=1 THEN LET h=0: GO SUB 8600
1025 PRINT AT a,b; INK i;s$
1030 IF bf THEN GO SUB 5000
1035 IF mf THEN GO SUB 6000
1040 GO SUB 100
1045 LET b=b+1: IF b=30 THEN PRINT AT a,30;CHR$ 32;CHR$ 32:
     GO TO 1000
1050 GO SUB 100
1055 GO TO 1015
5000 PRINT AT bx,by;CHR$ 32: LET bx=bx+1: LET by=by+y
5005 IF by<0 OR by>31 THEN LET by=by-y
5010 IF bx=22 THEN GO TO 5050
5015 PRINT AT bx,by;".": RETURN
5050 LET h=0: IF ABS (by-x)<=1 THEN LET by=x: LET h=1:
     LET t=t+1: PRINT AT 1,32-LEN STR$ t; PAPER 8;t
5055 LET bx=bx-1: FOR j=7 TO 1 STEP -1: PRINT AT bx,by;
     INK j;"*": NEXT j
5060 BEEP h+.01,50
5065 LET bf=0: RETURN
6000 IF mf=1 THEN LET mx=20: LET my=x
6005 PRINT AT mx,my;CHR$ 32: LET mx=mx-1: IF SCREEN$
     (mx,my)=CHR$ 46 OR mx=2 THEN GO TO 6050
6010 PRINT AT mx,my;"↑"
6015 IF mx<>a THEN GO TO 6040
6020 IF my<>b+2 THEN GO TO 6040
6025 LET s=s+1: FOR j=6 TO 1 STEP -1: PRINT AT a,b; INK j;
     "****": NEXT j: BEEP .5,30
6030 IF i=1 THEN LET s=s+4
6035 PRINT AT 1,0; PAPER 8;s: LET mf=-1: LET b=0
6040 LET mf=mf+1: RETURN
6050 LET mf=0: IF mx<>2  AND ATTR (mx,my)=8 THEN LET bf=0
6055 PRINT AT mx,my;CHR$ 32
6060 RETURN
7000 PRINT AT 1,12; FLASH 1; INK 2; PAPER 7;"GAME OVER":
     LET w=s
7005 IF t>s THEN LET w=t
7010 PRINT AT 1,(32- LEN STR$ t)*(t=w); FLASH 1; PAPER 7;
     INK 0;w
7015 IF t=s THEN PRINT AT 1,0; FLASH 1; PAPER 7; INK 0;s
7020 INPUT "PRESS ""ENTER"" TO RUN";s$
7025 RUN 10
8000 DATA 8,8,28,28,62,62,127,127,1,3,7,255,7,3,1,0,
     128,192,224,255,224,192,128,0
8500 FOR j=1 TO 10: PRINT AT INT (RND*18)+2,INT
     (RND*32); INK 7;".": NEXT j: RETURN
8600 PRINT AT 21,x; INK 6;CHR$ 144: RETURN
9000 SAVE "SAUCERS" LINE 0
```

FIREPOWER

Finally, a totally different type of space game.

In the previous three games, the TV screen gave you an armchair view of the action. In "Firepower," you are actually in control of your spaceship's laser gun, and the screen shows the view through your sights.

You have sixty seconds to shoot down as many enemy ships as you can by catching them directly in your sights (two points) or in the cross wires (one point).

A cross wire hit does *not* destroy the enemy, and therefore it *should* be possible to score:

Three points for every vertically traveling ship (by catching it first in your top cross-wire, and then, immediately afterwards, in the center of your sights.

Two points for every diagonally traveling ship, by *either* making a direct hit, *or* catching it with two successive cross-wire shots. (The first method is preferable, as otherwise you will still not have destroyed the ship even after the second hit, and you will waste time waiting for it to reach the end of the screen.)

You *cannot* outrun the enemy in this game, so positioning is of paramount importance. Do not chase forlornly after distant ships, but concentrate on reaching a strategic position ready for the next one.

Use keys "5," "6," "7" and "8" to move your sights. Use key "0" to fire *only* for cross-wire shots. Firing is automatic when you have a ship directly in your sights.

Program Notes

There is one User Defined Graphic only: the enemy ship.

The sights are formed by the four characters in array a$(). The rest of the array is empty, so that printing the entire array causes the cross-wires to appear on the screen.

The timing is achieved by lines 35 (to initialize), 100 and 105. As in all programs which use the System Variable FRAMES for accurate timing, the division factor in line 100 should be equivalent to your AC outlet frequency (see note on page XX).

FIREPOWER

```
5 FOR j=USR CHR$ 144 TO USR CHR$ 144+7: READ a: POKE j,a:
       NEXT j
10 DIM a$(65): LET a$(1)=CHR$ 124: LET a$(32)=CHR$ 45:
       LET a$(34)=CHR$ 45: LET a$(65)=CHR$ 124
15 BORDER 5: PAPER 5: INK 0: OVER 1: CLS
20 FOR j=1 TO 50: PRINT AT INT (RND*22),INT (RND*32);
       "*": NEXT j
25 LET s=0
30 LET x=11: LET y=15
35 POKE 23673,0: POKE 23672,0
40 LET t=0
45 LET b=0
100 LET t1=INT ((PEEK 23673*256+PEEK 23672)/60)
105 IF t<>t1 THEN BEEP .01,t: LET t=t1
110 PRINT AT 0,0; OVER 0;"SCORE ";s,"TIME ";t
115 IF t>=60 THEN GO TO 1000
120 IF NOT b THEN LET b=INT (RND*31)+1: LET a=1: LET
       d=INT (RND*3)-1: GO TO 130
125 PRINT AT a,b;CHR$ 144: LET a=a+1: LET b=b+d
130 IF a=21 OR b=0 OR b=32 THEN LET b=0: GO TO 200
135 PRINT AT a,b; INK 6;CHR$ 144
200 PRINT AT x,y; INK 8;a$
205 LET p=(x+1)*22+y: LET p1=a*22+b: IF p=p1 THEN BEEP
       1,50: LET s=s+2: PRINT AT a,b;CHR$ 144: LET b=0:
       GO TO 220
210 IF INKEY$<>"0" THEN GO TO 220
215 IF ABS (p-p1)=1 OR ABS (p-p1)=22 THEN BEEP .5,50:
       LET s=s+1
220 LET x1=x+(INKEY$="6" AND x<19)-(INKEY$="7" AND x>0)
225 LET y1=y+(INKEY$="8" AND y<30)-(INKEY$="5" AND y>1)
230 PRINT AT x,y; INK 8;a$
235 LET x=x1: LET y=y1
240 GO TO 100
1000 PRINT OVER 0; FLASH 1; PAPER 2; INK 7;AT 10,12;
       "GAME OVER"; FLASH 0;AT 21,5;"PRESS ""R"" TO
       PLAY AGAIN"
1005 IF INKEY$="r" THEN RUN
1010 GO TO 1005
5000 DATA 0,60,126,126,126,126,60,0
9000 SAVE "FIREPOWER" LINE 0
```